I0517390

Prayers for
Southern Seasons

Poems and prayers
for Christian worship and devotions

Joy Kingsbury-Aitken

Philip
Garside
Publishing Ltd.

When doing so please credit:
Joy Kingsbury-Aitken — Prayers for Southern Seasons (2019)

Contact Joy at
email: jmk_dsa@hotmail.com

For David

Paperback International edition 2023:
ISBN 9781991027443

Also available
Paperback New Zealand: ISBN 9781988572086
Paperback print-on-demand USA: ISBN 9781095952924
PDF: ISBN 9781988572093
ePub: ISBN 97819885721096
Kindle/Mobi: ISBN 9781988572116

Philip Garside Publishing Ltd
PO Box 17160
Wellington 6147
New Zealand

books@pgpl.co.nz — www.philipgarsidebooks.com

Cover photo:
Alexander Garside—Garside Imaging
(From Colonial Knob above Tawa,
looking over Cook Strait to the South Island)

Contents

Definitions

Gathering: prayers for commencing worship, calls to worship.

Candle lighting: prayers for the ritual of lighting of candles.

Thanksgiving: prayers that praise and thank God for his provision.

Intercession: prayers for others, and for us in relation to others.

Petition: prayers for ourselves, the church.

Confession: prayers of contrition.

Assurance: prayers affirming confidence in God's forgiveness.

Illumination: prayers for understanding the scriptures.

Offering: prayers dedicating gifts for the work of the church.

Blessing: benedictions.

Commissioning: concluding prayers, sending forth.

Poetry: meditations in the form of poems.

Prayers with lines in ***bold italic*** type can be read responsively.

Introduction

Since my ministry as a lay preacher began about thirteen years ago, I have been aware that to lead a congregation in worship is both a great privilege and a great responsibility. Prayer is a vital part of public worship. Most of the prayers included in this book were written for services I have been invited to lead. Subsequently some have been shared with fellow lay worship leaders, whose enthusiasm for my liturgical writing encouraged me to compile this anthology.

Here in Aotearoa New Zealand the church year begins in early summer, harvest comes during the fast of Lent, and we celebrate Easter not when life is emerging anew in a burst of spring flowering but when leaves are turning red and gold and falling to the ground. The traditional seasonal symbolism associated with the church's major festivals, which works so well in the northern hemisphere, has limited meaning for us folk who live south of the equator. The prayers and poems in this collection have been arranged to reflect the cycle of the seasons as we experience them, and the church's feasts and fasts, and other commemorations, as they occur within those seasons.

Congregational participation is invited through a responsive reading of many of the prayers, and worship will be enhanced by recognition of the rich vein of Biblical storytelling and imagery that has been drawn upon. Also included are poems intended for personal reflection. These are more suitable for printing on the front cover of an order of service or within a church bulletin than for use in public worship.

My hope is that this book will be a useful resource for worship leaders, providing just the right words when they need them, and that they, and others who happen to open these pages, may find within sparks of inspiration to ignite their own devotional creativity.

I would like to thank the many congregations who have invited me to lead them in worship, and keep inviting me back, for their encouragement and constructive advice. Most of all I would like to thank my husband David for his considerable on-going support of my involvement in lay preaching.

Joy Kingsbury-Aitken
Easter 2019

Summer

Summer Thanksgiving (Thanksgiving)

The beach and the bach call us in summer
to come away from our work and our daily routines;
to come away and play, be like children again,
and make happy memories during warm, sunny days.
Thank God for summer and for our summer holidays.

The farm and the orchard call us in summer
to make hay and silage while the sun's brightly shining;
to harvest the fruit that is now sweetly ripening,
and so reap and enjoy the rich bounty of earth.
Thank God for summer and for summer's abundance.

Garden and barbecue call us in summer
to entertain friends, family and neighbours
to share festive food and drink that make merry,
and in summer's warmth to celebrate Christmas.
Thank God for the past year and for the year that is coming.

Thank God for our work and for times of refreshing.
Thank God for the earth sustaining our living.
Thank God for the family and friends that we have.
Thank God for the seasons each with its riches.
Thank God for summer, and for summer's pleasures.
Thank God.

Advent

The God of Love Came as a Gift of Love (Blessing)

During Advent we recall how the God of love
came into the world as a gift of love.
We remember that God is faithful,
may his gospel fill you with hope.
We remember that God is merciful,
may his compassion fill you with peace.
We remember that God is bountiful,
may his grace fill you with joy.
The overflowing blessings of God,
Father, Son and Holy Spirit,
be poured out upon you, and upon your family and friends,
during this the season of great joy,
and throughout the year to come. Amen.

Advent is... (Poetry)

Advent is the season of early fruitfulness,
of new potatoes, fresh strawberries, ripe cherries.
The season of busy preparation,
of buying gifts, baking treats, inviting guests.
The season of anticipation
of summer holidays, back yard barbecues, beach volleyball.
The season of year endings,
of school prize-giving, festive parties, work functions.

Advent, the season of tawdry tinsel and silly shop music.
Who actually is dreaming of a white Christmas?
No sleigh rides in the snow for us thank you.
We're south of the equator, and its summertime!

Advent is the season of year beginnings,
the liturgical cycle starting afresh,
with candles lit and carols sung.
The season of remembrance and of anticipation
of looking back, looking for, looking forward
to Messiah who came, who comes, and will come again.

The season of preparation,
of roles allocated, costumes improvised,
manger ready, annual re-enactment of nativity,
celebration of incarnation.
The season of eternal fruitfulness,
blessed gratitude for the Spirit's gifts,
for peace and hope and joy and love.

Advent, the season full of immense mystery
and meaning transcending winter images,
and ancient traditions brought from afar.
Let's celebrate,
for summer has arrived for us southern folk,
and with it is coming Christmas!

Gathering in Hope (Gathering)

Romans 5:3, Matthew 18:20

Gracious God, it is hope that gathers us together here,
your people come to worship you this Advent season.
Hope that came as an infant born in a borrowed room.
Hope that comes through his life story
retold to each new generation.
Hope that comes in his teaching
challenging us to become greater than we think we can be.
Hope that comes with his love demonstrated by his self-giving
challenging us to also give our lives in service to others.
Hope that comes with his promise
of being the unseen presence among us
when in twos and threes we get together.

Gracious God because your love has been poured
into our hearts by the spirit Christ has given us,
we have a hope that cannot disappoint,
and it is that hope that calls us here
to worship you in this season of anticipation.
We have left for a moment the cacophony of our world
with its busy festival preparations,
to come and sit quietly and listen for your still small voice.
Speak softly to us today and bless our speaking to you we pray. Amen.

Giving Gifts of Love (Offering)

1 John 4:7-8

Receive these gifts,
small tokens of our love,
our grateful acknowledgement
of your great gift of love;
the One who is God Incarnate,
Perfect Sacrifice, Risen Christ, Son,
who came, and comes, and will come again.
Accept these gifts, small tokens of our love,
and use them for his work of love. Amen.

Lighting the Advent Candles (Candle lighting)

We enter the Season of Advent focused on hope.
Hope that our present devotional labours
will lead to future spiritual successes.
Hope that our current troublesome cares
will give way to joyful celebrations.
Hope that our anticipation of incarnation
will ignite anew our appreciation
of the old and ever new story of nativity.
We begin the Season of Advent with hope
and so light the first Advent candle,
looking forward to Christmas. (Amen)

We observe the Season of Advent thankful for peace.
The spirit of peace within the church
and the peace we share with family and friends.
The peace we enjoy within a free nation,
the peace we hope will one day be worldwide.
The peace of mind and spirit
that surpasses understanding,
being the peace we have in and through Christ Jesus.
We observe the Season of Advent in peace
and so we light the second Advent candle,
looking forward to Christmas. (Amen)

We celebrate the Season of Advent filled with immense joy.
The joy we feel in the company of others
gathered around dinner tables and at summer barbecues.
The joy sung forth in carols traditional and new,
telling of the joy of a firstborn son,
child of Mary, child of God.
The joy proclaimed through the gospel message
about a Saviour who came and is coming again.
We celebrate the Season of Advent with joy
and light the third Advent candle
looking forward to Christmas. (Amen)

We embrace the Season of Advent by giving and receiving love.
Love bestowed on those who enrich our lives.
Love felt within the community of faith.
Love expressed to the One who epitomises love.
We are enfolded in God's love for all humanity,
for whom Jesus was born in Bethlehem,
died on Golgotha's lonely hill,
and rose to glory in Jerusalem.
We embrace the Season of Advent with love
and light the fourth Advent candle
looking forward to Christmas. (Amen)

We rejoice in our celebration of God's redemptive grace.
Rereading familiar scriptures and singing again old songs
that tell the human story of divine incarnation;
of a family caught up in an empire-wide census,
of a baby boy cradled in a manger,
of shepherds startled by a host of angels,
and learned men bringing gifts from afar.
Like them we pay homage to our God and Saviour.
So endowed by Israel's Eternal King
with the Spirit of hope and peace, joy and love
we light the Christ candle for Christmas has come. Amen.

The Season of Our Joy (Gathering)

Isaiah 9:6-7, Luke 2:10, John 1:1-3, 14; John 3:16-17; 14:27;
Philippians 4:7

The Season of Advent is the season of our joy,
the season of rejoicing for the guidance of the Wonderful
Counsellor, the Word who was in the beginning with God,
who became flesh and lived among us.

The Season of Advent is the season of our joy,
the season of worship of you Mighty God,
our Everlasting Father, who sent the Son into the world
not to condemn the world but to save it.

The Season of Advent is the season of our joy,
the season for proclaiming the coming of the Prince of Peace,
whose gives an everlasting peace that cannot be destroyed
by the circumstances of our lives.

We rejoice in the coming of the Christ,
the helpless baby in a manger in Bethlehem,
the crucified saviour on a hill in Jerusalem,
the glorious Alpha and Omega,
who is the first and the last, the beginning and the end.

We rejoice and praise you Almighty God. Amen.

The Season of Advent (Confession)

Lord, when the dark thoughts of despair begin to trouble our minds
bring to our remembrance that we have much to hope for.
The Season of Advent is a season of hope.

Lord, when we get caught up in troubles and strife
bring to mind the power of conciliation and wise words gently spoken.
The Season of Advent is a season of peace.

Lord, when sorrow and sadness threaten to engulf us
help us hold on to the gladness we have in our assurance of salvation.
The Season of Advent is a season of joy.

Lord, when discord and animosity enter our lives
help us to be people of harmony and goodwill.
The Season of Advent is a season of love.

Lord, forgive us our sins, help us overcome our failings,
teach us to forgive each other and to forgive ourselves.
The Season of Advent is a season of grace.

Lord, as we rush our way towards Christmas
help us to be bringers of the gift of selfless caring.
The Season of Advent is a season for sharing.

Lord, may this season of Advent bring with it hope,
the promise of peace, and the experience of joy; and most of all
may this season of Advent be a season of love. Amen.

What a Gift! (Gathering)

What a gift you gave us
through the birth of a baby boy.
What a hope you gave us,
what peace, what love, what joy.

This is why we gather
to celebrate his birth,
to thank you for the saviour
your gift of enormous worth.

No bags of gold or silver,
no frankincense and myrrh
could us from death deliver
and bring us to new birth.

Only the gift you gave us,
your beloved incarnate son,
only his life could save us
from what we had become.

This is why we gather
to celebrate his birth,
to thank you for the saviour,
your gift of tremendous worth. Amen.

Gather Us Together this Holy Morning Lord (Gathering)

John 16:33; Isaiah 9:6

Gather us together this holy morning Lord,
with minds focused on praising you,
hearts focused on loving your people,
hands eager to help one another.
Gather us together this holy morning Lord,
with minds open to learning your truth,
hearts open to receiving your love,
hands eager for doing your bidding.

Gather us together this holy morning Lord,
with minds joyful in your presence,
with hearts thankful for your peace,
with hands happy to serve you always.
Gather us together this holy morning Lord,
that with our minds and hearts and hands
we may truly worship you, Wonderful Counsellor,
Mighty God, Everlasting Father, Prince of Peace.
Gather us together. Amen.

Light has come into the World (Gathering)

Isaiah 9:2; John 1:4-5, 9; 12:36

Light has come into the world.
Greater than the globes glowing down on city streets,
lovelier than the twinkling baubles strung around Christmas trees,
stronger than the twilight that lingers late on summer evenings.
A light never switched off and which darkness never overcomes.

Light has come into the world.
Replacing the darkness of despair with the brightness of hope,
overcoming the shadows of strife with the splendour of peace,
replacing the gloom of sorrow with the sparkle of joy,
eliminating the blackness of hate by the radiance of love.

Light has come into the world.
The Eternal Light. The Christ Light.
We who once dwelt in darkness now walk in the light of his life.
His light shines down, around and through us gathered here,
who by believing in him have become his children of light. Amen.

Epiphany

We Gather as Pilgrims (Gathering)

Hebrews 12:22

We speak of the Christian calling as a pilgrimage;
a journey towards understanding what it truly means to follow Jesus.
As fellow travellers we gather together today
to discover what it really means to be led by your presence
through the wilderness of our world;
to discover what it really means to be guided by your Spirit
towards the fullness of your kingdom
and the realisation of our citizenship
in a heavenly city not of human making.

May our worship today be acceptable to you,
may it refresh and strengthen us as we go forth
on the next stage of this sacred journey,
which we have been called by you to make
as individuals within a community of believers.
We who are gathered here today
seek your blessing on this gathering
and on each person present. Amen.

Blessing for Pilgrims (Blessing)

May you perceive
God's supporting presence
in everything you do,
everywhere you go,
in everyone you meet,
and in everything you encounter,
every day of your life;
and may God, Father, Son and Spirit,
bless you and guide you
and those who travel with you
on your earthly pilgrimage,
this day, and during all the days ahead. Amen.

We Bring Our Gifts (Offering)

We bring our gifts in gratitude for the generosity of God.
We bring our gifts in expectation
that they will be used for the work of God.
We bring our gifts in love for the people of God.
We bring our gifts asking for God's blessing upon them. Amen.

We Have Been on a Journey (Poetry)

Matthew 2:1-12

We have been on a journey travelling
away from our usual dwelling place,
away from our everyday certainties,
away from the comfortably familiar.

We have been on a journey travelling
towards the place of pilgrimage,
towards perceptions that challenge,
towards the insecurity of the unknown.

We have been on a journey responding to
a prophecy – a promise of better things,
a star – a speck of light in the darkness of our being,
a dream – that somehow survived the reality of our waking.

We have been on a journey experiencing
despair, joy, wonder,
as we traversed across desolate deserts,
along verdant valleys,
through magnificent mountain passes.

We have been on a journey carrying
costly gifts,
signifying that the price of life is death.
Gold, frankincense, myrrh,
suitable tribute to bring to a king.

We have been on a journey
expecting to encounter a prince in a gilded palace,
instead we were led to
a peasant boy in a borrowed room.
Such is the paradox of God!

We ask ourselves,
were we fools, are we now wise?
We can't say.
As we turn homewards,
returning by a different way,
all we know for sure is this
we have been changed!

Travelling God (Intercession)

Father, you are the travelling God.
You travelled with Abraham from Chaldea to Canaan.
You travelled with the Children of Israel from the land of bondage
to the land of promise by way of the wilderness.
You travelled westward with the wise men to Bethlehem
and southward with Jesus on his fateful journey to Jerusalem.

Lord you travel with us on our journey of life.
In our oasis times of plenty you are there.
In our desert times of need you are there.
When we turn towards you,
and when we turn away from you, you are there.
We praise and thank you for your steadfast faithfulness.

Father, you are full of mercy and loving kindness.
We entrust to your care family and friends
who are currently stumbling along rocky roads
and struggling to climb to the summits of steep hills.
Encourage, comfort, deliver and heal
those whom we worry about at this time.
Transform fear into faith, despair into hope, and sighing into singing.

Lord we remember and bring before you
those suffering from the horrors of civil war,
those suffering from the horrors of famine,
those suffering from the evils of government corruption
and financial mismanagement,
and all others whose suffering is great
but which hardly registers in the news media,
and when it does is quickly forgotten by us.

Father you travel with us, but you don't walk for us.
You do for us only what we cannot do for ourselves,
so transform us God so that as individuals,
communities and countries
we will all take much better care of one another
during this our time of earthly pilgrimage.
Make us instruments of your peace. Amen.

Autumn

A Season of Transition (Poetry)

Summer is past, winter draws near,
autumn is a season of transition.
A time of preparation.
Epiphany is past, Easter draws near,
Lent is a season of transition.
A time of preparation.

The story is told of Jesus walking southwards
taking fateful steps from Galilee to Judaea.
A time of determination.
The story is told of disciples shocked and rejecting
predictions of death and resurrection.
A time of incomprehension.

Pilgrims excited, Passover coming,
commemorating past, anticipating future deliverance.
A time of celebration.
Chief priests worried, Passover coming,
remembering past, fearing future disturbances.
A time of apprehension.

Soldiers marching, Governor resplendent,
putting on display the might of mighty Rome.
A time of intimidation.
Man on a donkey, crowds shouting, "Save Us,"
waving palm fronds and throwing down their cloaks.
A time of acclamation.

A final supper, bread and wine shared,
words of encouragement followed by despair.
A time of betrayal and desertion.
Man crowned with thorns, hung on a cross,
words of forgiveness and promise spoken.
A time of suffering and sacrifice.

Women confused and afraid,
grave empty, angels present.
A time of hope slowly dawning.
A stranger joins mourners on the road to Emmaus,
his identity discovered in the breaking of bread.
A time of revelation.

Harvest

God of Creation, God of Harvest (Thanksgiving)

Genesis 2:15

God of Creation, God of harvest
these are the days of thanksgiving –
for grass cut and baled,
wrapped and stored to feed flocks and herds,
source of meat and milk;
for grains of barley and wheat poured into silos,
waiting to be baked into bread and cakes;
for apples and apricots sorted in packing sheds,
dispatched to supermarkets far and wide.

God of Creation, God of harvest,
these are the days of thanksgiving –
for the minerals and microbes,
the sunshine and moisture,
that you blend together to bring forth abundance.
From out of the fragile ecosystems of your creation,
marvellous in its complexity and variety,
comes life supporting crops from the fields,
vegetables in gardens, fruit on trees.

God of Creation, God of harvest,
these are the days of thanksgiving –
for the garden you created east of Eden
and the ancestors you put there to tend it.
Our tasks haven't changed, only our location.
We thank you for agriculturalists and pastoralists
for gardeners and orchardists
and for the merchants who bring their produce to market.

God of Creation, God of harvest,
These are the days of thanksgiving –
for all that sustain us,
for all that inspires us,
for the bounty of your land
and the generosity of your Spirit,
we humbly offer our gratitude. Amen.

Thanksgiving for Food (Thanksgiving)

We thank you God for food.
The food that nourishes our bodies, giving us strength for living.
The food around which we gather, facilitating our fellowship.
The foods that taste sweet, bringing pleasure with each mouthful,
and the savoury foods, bringing spices into to our lives.

We thank you for the earth's fruitfulness.
For the fertility of the soil, for the moisture of the rain,
for the light and warmth of sunshine,
all required for plants to grow and animals to thrive.
We thank you for the seasons of planting, growing and harvesting,
and for the folk who do the planting, the tending and the harvesting.

We thank you God for food.
We are grateful we have enough food,
and are shocked that some go hungry.
Bless our offerings of autumn's abundance,
the food we bring to celebrate harvest festival.
May this food be a blessing for families in need.

In all seasons of the year, bless those who give,
and those who give out food from food banks,
and bless those to whom the food is given.
In a world of plenty none should go without.
We thank you God for food. Amen.

Lent

Change (Poetry)

God who created the possibility of change
when you exploded the universe into being,
setting in motion the forces that formed stars and planets
and led to the beginning of life, and eventually to us.
God who initiated change by coming into the world,
living our life, dying our death, and through resurrection
showing us the possibility of living anew,
of changing and being changed.
God, both immutable and transforming,
we have been changed by your love for us
and your love for us has changed you. Amen.

From the Ordinary and Everyday (Gathering)

From the ordinary and everyday and the delightfully different;
from times when we're been happy and hopeful,
and times when we're been sad and discouraged;
in an attitude of faith or in questioning uncertainty,
we come together to worship.

Open our minds to your majesty,
our spirits to your glory,
our souls to your loving kindness.
Bless our gathering this morning
with grace-filled transformation
on our pilgrimage together
through the holy season of Lent. Amen.

Our Imperfect Faith (Gathering)

Matthew 17:20; Mark 4:35-41

Lord God, we gather here today because of faith.
Not a perfect faith that knows no doubt,
not a powerful faith that moves mountains and still storms,
not a passionate faith that sets hearts afire for you.
Rather all too often ours is a wavering faith,
full of questions that go unanswered.
Ours is a fragile faith, tossed about
in the choppy waters of our life experiences.
Ours is a temperate faith, more gentle glow than blazing fire.

Increasingly we live among those who imagine faith to be irrelevant,
to be at best a crutch for those unwilling to face their own mortality.
We know differently, Lord, for we know you,
and in knowing you we have faith.
A faith that is not without flaws and weaknesses,
with periods of apathy, but nevertheless a faith,
inspired by your Spirit, that binds us to you,
affirmed by your love and our experience of resurrection.

So Lord, we gather here today because of faith,
and in doing so we seek your blessing on our worship today.
We seek the gift of a growing, glowing faith in you. Amen.

All Too Often (Confession)

Lord, all too often we are so attached to our way of doing things
that we close our minds to the possibility of doing things your way.
Forgive us.

Lord, all too often we are so attached to our point of view
that we close our eyes to the new insights you want to show us.
Forgive us.

Lord, all too often we are so attached to our style of living
that we close our ears to your call to discipleship,
or like Moses before the burning bush,
we are full of very good reasons
to excuse us from being of service to you.
Forgive us.

We often can clearly see when others are being foolish,
and are quick to judge them,
but are blind to our own lack of wisdom,
and are slow to change.
Forgive us.

We can also be overly occupied with our own problems,
and too little concerned about the struggles of others.
Forgive us.

Lord this is the season of Lent,
when our thoughts turn once more to Easter
and to the old, old story of crucifixion and resurrection;
a story of loss that was gain, of defeat that was victory,
of death that became eternal life.

We acknowledge the mysterious wisdom of your ways,
and we ask that in forgiving us our failures,
you help us glimpse your bigger vision for our lives,
and that you instil within us some of your wonderful wisdom.
We ask this in Jesus' name. Amen.

Forgive Us, Restore Us and Change Us (Confession)

Lord, your intention is that we be family,
kindly, self-sacrificing, loving.
Sometimes we act more like enemies,
uncaring, self-serving, unintentionally cruel.
In such times forgive us, restore us and change us.

Lord, your intention is that we be generous,
sharing the bounty you have provided.
Sometimes we act more like misers,
reserving your blessing for ourselves alone.
In such times forgive us, restore us and change us.

Lord, your intention is that we be worshipful,
giving you glory, praising you for your grace.
Sometimes we act as if you don't matter,
by going our own ways, doing our own things.
In such times forgive us, restore us and change us.

Lord we thank you for your parental care
and are grateful for your brotherly love.
Lord we thank you for your liberality
in providing our needs and much more besides.
Lord we thank you for your faithfulness
that never wanes irrespective of our waywardness.

Lord your mightiness humbles us.
Your promises elevate us.
Your sacrifice has saved us.
So we come with words of praise and thanksgiving,
knowing that you have forgiven and restored us,
and that you are changing us. Amen.

God of Abraham (Gathering)

God of Abraham, father of the faithful,
God of Isaac, son of promise,

God of Jacob, usurper and wrestler,
God of Jesus, Messiah and Saviour;

it is you we come to worship,
having inherited an ancient tradition.

It is you we come to worship,
in new ways relevant for modern life.

It is you we come to worship,
and in our coming we seek your blessing
on all gathered here before you today. Amen.

In Lent We Have a Tradition (Intercession)

Isaiah 58

Lord God, in Lent we have a tradition of going without,
of making small sacrifices for spiritual gain.

We live among those for whom going without is not a choice.
In our community are people who are hungry,
who are homeless, who are cold and in trouble.

Lord God you say that the fasting you want
is for us to share our food with the hungry,
provide shelter for the homeless,
give clothes to those who need them,
and relieve the oppressed of their burdens.

Lord God help us to do these things.
Help us to be a compassionate people.
Help us to become helpers of those in need.

In Lent we have a tradition of retelling the story of Jesus,
of how he said blessings await the poor and sorrows the rich,
and how he was crucified for speaking truth to power.

We live in a world where people become rich by exploiting the poor,
and where journalists are imprisoned, and even murdered,
for revealing the corruption of self-serving rulers.

Lord God you say that the fasting you want
is for us to lighten the burden of those who labour too long and too hard,
to ensure everyone is paid a wage they can live on,
to support the victims of abuse and to release the wrongfully imprisoned.

Lord God help us to do these things.
Help us be champions of truth and justice.
Help us to become helpers of those in need.

In Lent we have a tradition of reflecting on the Scriptures
and as Easter approaches of repenting of our sins that cause strife.

We live in a world where lies spread rapidly on social media
and the reputations of the innocent are quickly destroyed.
In our world unimaginable suffering is being caused
by the bullets and bombs of those who pursue war.

Lord God you say that the fasting you want
is for us to cease being judgemental and to stop spreading rumours,
to put an end to the quarrelling and fighting among us,
to make the refugee welcome and to help the distressed.

Lord God help us to do these things.
Help us to become peace promoting people.
Helps us to become helpers of those in need. Amen.

Transfiguration Sunday

Keep Us Moving (Petition)

Matthew 17:1-8; Mark 9:2-8; Luke 9:28-36

God who appeared as cloud and fire to a slave people
traversing desert lands in the shadow of Sinai;
God who appeared as a whispering voice to a hunted prophet
seeking safety in a cave high up on Sinai;
God who took on the limits of humanity but who appeared
in glorious divinity to disciples experiencing anew
your transforming presence as at Sinai;
it is you we address with our words of praise and our words of petition.

God guide us through our wilderness experiences.
Grant us the confidence to keep following you when the way is gruelling,
the journeying long and the destination uncertain.
Just like the Israelites we too often become fretful
and anxious and lose our faith in you.
Still our fears and keep us moving
on our journey through Lent and through life.

God comfort us when we are disheartened, afraid and alone.
Not with big gestures that would frighten us
but in quiet moments grant us the assurance of your presence.
Just like the prophets we too often feel your demands are too daunting and
too difficult for us, and we want to run away and hide.
Calm us, encourage us and keep us moving
on our journey through Lent and through life.

God reassure us when we face a pending crisis.
Grant us the ability to see beyond the present moment
to a future full of hope and promise.
Just like the disciples we too can be deceived into thinking that we
can achieve your goals by the easy pathways we much prefer to take.
Strengthen us, reorient us and keep us moving,
on our journey through Lent and through life.

God, we have come to a new Sinai, the mount of transfiguration.
We have come seeking to be transformed.
Forgive us, embolden us and change us continually into being all that you intend us to be, all that we could possibly be.
Not bound by our weaknesses but freed by your grace.
God of cloud and fire, small voice and loud,
God of majestic glory cloaked in the unremarkable commonplace,
guide us and comfort us, reassure us and reorient us
so that we may continue daily our journeying with you.
God keep us moving we pray throughout Lent and throughout life. Amen.

Palm (Passion) Sunday

Praise the One who Came in the Name of the Lord (Gathering)

John 12:12-15

Praise the one who came in the name of the Lord.
Praise the one who came to save us.

Praise Him who descended to his destiny in Jerusalem.
Praise Him who did not flinch from the suffering to come.

They gave thanks for the one sent by the Lord.
They sang hosanna to the one sent to save them.

They welcomed their king with waving palm fronds.
They chose him to be their Passover sacrifice.

We give thanks for the beloved of the Lord.
We give thanks for him shedding his glory.

We give thanks for the anointed suffering servant.
We give thanks for his ride towards his cross.

Praise him whose name is Christ the Lord.
Praise him who is our Saviour.

Praise him who died and lives again.
Praise him our eternal Redeemer. Amen

Like Passover Pilgrims (Gathering)

Matthew 21:1-10; John 12:12-16; Isaiah 53:10

Like Passover pilgrims
descending towards the holy city
crying out, "save us now,"
we too cry hosanna, needing salvation,
as we commence
the journey of holy week
towards cross and tomb,
as we seek to comprehend once more
the horror of crucifixion
and the mystery of resurrection.

Like palm waving disciples
escorting the man on a donkey
shouting, "blessed is he who comes in the name of the Lord,"
we too sing words of jubilation, to welcome
this anointed one who came for them
and yet comes again for us,
who had power yet chose weakness for us,
who died and yet lives for us,
enduring the terror of the cross
for the mystery of an empty tomb.

Like ancient Israelites in occupied Judaea
rejoicing that their long expected Messiah
is now riding towards Jerusalem,
in accordance with ancient prophecies,
we too rejoice in the current reign of this servant king,
while eagerly anticipating his promised future coming.
His life was proclaimed an offering for sin,
yet we remain oppressed in a sin-occupied world.
Crucified and risen one, we also cry out to you,
"Hosanna to the Son of David…
Hosanna in the highest heaven!" Amen.

God Our Temple (Poetry)

Malachi 3:1; Luke 19:45-46; 21:5-6; John 4:20-21; 7:37-38;
Ephesians 21:19-22; 1 Peter 2:9; Revelation 21:22

You came to the temple suddenly,
as the prophet Malachi said you would,
you saw it was a den of thieves,
and not a house of prayer to God.
The most glorious sacred precinct, the largest under Roman rule,
was the temple in Jerusalem which you said was doomed to fall.
You said to the Samaritan woman that the time had already come
to no longer worship in Jerusalem or on Mount Gerizim.
In the temple on a feast day during a ceremony seeking rain,
you cried out to all who thirst to come to you and be sustained.
For Lord, you and God Almighty are yourselves the sacred space,
from which flows a mighty river, the Holy Spirit with gifts of grace.

Now you are forming us Lord Jesus into a house of living stones,
built on prophets and apostles, yourself the cornerstone.
Cleanse and perfect us Lord Jesus, make us worthy of our role
in the temple you are forming where your glory comes to dwell.
So we come to you Lord Jesus as you invited us to do,
to drink the living waters that from deep within you flow.
Make of us a royal priesthood, form from us God's holy nation,
that we may proclaim your mighty acts,
Jesus Christ source of salvation. Amen.

We have Heard Your Call (Gathering)

We have heard your call Lord
to assemble in this place to worship.
We have counted the cost Lord
of being committed to a life of worship.

We are building your temple Lord
of worshipping saints whose foundation is Christ.
We are aware of your presence among us Lord,
and we seek your blessing on our time of Worship.
Amen.

Tuesday before Easter

The Size of the Gift (Poetry)

Mark 12:41-44

It's not the size of the gift that's important,
but the love with which it is given.
It's not the value of the money donated
but the sacrifice made by the giver.
It's not the honour the rich men sought
but the humility the poor woman possessed.

Jesus sat opposite the treasury,
watching people drop their gifts into it.
The many coins of the rich rattled loudly
down the funnel and into the box.
Then came a poor widow who gave
to the temple two small copper coins.

Jesus turned to his disciples and said,
"See what this widow has done.
Many have given large offerings today
but she has given more than them all.
The rich have given from their abundance
but in her poverty she has given her all."

It's the size of the gift that's important
when the gift is a human life.
It's a gift of immeasurable value
when the sacrifice is the Son of God.
It's a gift of great love and great honour
when in humility Jesus died for us all.

Given in faith (Offering)

Lord, our offerings are an expression of our faith.
We have faith that you notice our gifts.
We have faith that you will use our gifts.
We have faith that good will come from our gifts.
We give out of our gratitude for your gifts to us,
including the gift of our faith in you.
Bless these gifts and may they be a blessing to others. Amen.

Pray for the Peace of Jerusalem (Poetry)

Psalm 122:6; 2 Samuel 5:6-12; 1 Kings 8:10-13; Isaiah 65:18;
Malachi 3:1-2; Matthew 23:9-14; Luke 20: 41-44; 21:20-24

Called to be the City of Peace,
Jerusalem's legacy has been strife and war.
Called to be a place of joy,
Jerusalem's experience has been pain and grief.
Intended to be the City of God
Jerusalem is where the prophets were killed.
Pray for the peace of Jerusalem.

David captured the Jebusite stronghold,
which he then renamed after himself.
From Zion David reigned over all Israel
in a palace of cedar built by Hiram of Tyre.
Solomon was chosen to be his successor
and in Jerusalem he built a temple for God.
The glory of the Lord filled the house of the Lord.
Pray for the peace of Jerusalem.

But Jerusalem became a place of corruption.
Instead of seeking justice her leaders oppressed.
God sent prophets to warn of the consequences
of doing evil instead of upholding what's good.
For the Lord of hosts is exalted by justice
and shows himself holy by his righteousness.
Pray for the peace of Jerusalem.

Nebuchadnezzar destroyed Solomon's temple.
Nehemiah ensured that a new temple was built.
Antiochus the Syrian polluted this temple,
provoking the Jews to rise up in revolt.
Herod the Great made the temple site grander,
and to this temple came the Lord that they sought.
But they could not endure the day of his coming.
Pray for the peace of Jerusalem.

Jesus gazed down upon the holy city,
its temple sparkling in the morning sunlight,
and Jesus lamented over Jerusalem,
"How often I desired to gather your children
like a hen sheltering chicks under her wings."
Desolation is coming to a people not willing
to welcome the one who comes in the name of the Lord.
Pray for the peace of Jerusalem.

Titus gazed down upon the rebel city,
its temple sparkling in the morning sunlight.
Titus plotted how to capture the city
and punish the Jews who resisted Rome's rule.
Soon it would be a city on fire,
its people slaughtered, its temple destroyed,
with no one to welcome in the name of the Lord.
Pray for the peace of Jerusalem.

The temple has gone and none has replaced it.
The Dome of the Rock is where it once stood.
A city now sacred to three faith traditions
is a city of peace with no peace in sight.
Pray for the Israelis and for the Palestinians
and for the day when everyone will say,
"Blessed is he who comes in the name of the Lord."
Pray for the peace of Jerusalem.

Who Is this Man? (Poetry)

Who is this man who walks the roads of Galilee,
attracting crowds wherever he goes?
This story-teller, this healer, this peasant,
who debates Torah with the experts.

Who is this man who dines with Pharisees and sinners,
choosing fishermen and tax collectors for disciples?
This rabbi, this sage, this scandalous man,
who claims he has authority to forgive sin.

Who is this man who comes to Jerusalem
alarming chief priests and Roman governor?
This pilgrim, this prophet, this martyr Messiah,
foretelling the destruction of Israel,
while Israel's leaders plot his demise. Who is this man?

Maundy Thursday

Grubby Feet (Confession)

John 13:1-11, Isaiah 1:18

Lord we enter your presence with grubby feet,
made dirty with the messiness of our lives.
Feet which have often plodded reluctantly towards you
in response to your call to us,
feet that have tap danced quickly away from you
in pursuit of our own desires;
feet which have strayed into dark alleyways
far from the path of righteousness illuminated by your Word
feet that have stumbled into murky places
and got stuck where we don't want to be.

Our good intentions and our desire
is to always travel wisely and well and with you Lord,
but our experience confirms the truth of Jesus' observation
that the gateway to a God-centred life is very narrow
and the road is often difficult. None of us can travel it alone.
Indeed it is only by keeping our eyes on Jesus,
who is the way to truth and life, and following where he leads,
that we can tread the kingdom highway.

Lord we are travel stained and in need of refreshing.
Bring again the healing waters of our baptism.
Though we be blotched scarlet with our sins,
you offer to wash us as white as freshly fallen snow.
We thank you for your steadfast and abounding love,
and for your forgiving cleansing that is always available to us. Amen.

Gifts for the World (Offering)

John 17

Grace bestowing God,
you have gifted us to Christ
and in turn we gift to you
these offerings in the hope
that they will glorify your name.
You called us from the world
to do your work within the world,
and so we bring to you these gifts
to be a blessing for the world. Amen.

Good Friday

Darkest of Days (Poetry)

He was just another troublesome Jew,
or so Pilate and the chief priests thought.
He was just another would-be messiah
whose kingdom would soon come to naught.

A bounty of silver was placed on his head.
The betrayer was one of his own.
In the darkness of night to Jesus he led
the temple police and soldiers of Rome.

In fear his disciples scattered like sheep
when their shepherd was taken away.
A repentant Peter later would weep
after denying him three times that day.

First a Jewish hearing and then the trial
over which Rome's Prefect presided,
being falsely accused by men full of guile
the sentence they sought soon decided.

Injustice prevailed on this darkest of days,
Rome's power would not be denied.
This man who could be the king of the Jews
was first scourged and then crucified.

His story is told over and over again
as it didn't end with his death on the cross.
For this crucified man rose forever to reign
as Lord God of the whole universe.

We Remember Your Suffering (Praise & Confession)

John 18 & 19

Lord Jesus Christ, today we remember your suffering,
the injustice of your trial, the cruelty of your execution.
Today we acknowledge with a heavy heart
that people are still being tried unjustly and punished with callousness.

Lord Jesus Christ, today we remember how you were betrayed
by a close friend conspiring with the religious leaders of your day.
Today we acknowledge with immense shame
that people are still being betrayed by ecclesiastical power.

Lord Jesus Christ, today we remember how you were deserted
by your disciples who ran for their lives when you were arrested.
Today we acknowledge with mortification
that you are still being abandoned when fear overwhelms faith.

Lord Jesus Christ, today we remember your courage,
your resolve to remain faithful, your dignity before Pilate.
Today we acknowledge with great sadness
that people are still being persecuted for being people of faith.

Lord Jesus Christ, today we remember how you were mocked
by the soldiers of Rome who crowned you with thorns.
Today we acknowledge with indignity
that people are still being mocked for being servants of God.

Lord Jesus Christ, today we remember your cross,
the instrument of torture you were nailed to.
Today we acknowledge with horror
the great capacity we all have to be hideously cruel.

Lord Jesus Christ, today we remember the women
who stayed with you during the hours of your suffering.
Today we acknowledge with appreciation
the people who care for the distressed and the dying.

Lord Jesus Christ, today we remember how your friends mourned
and gave you a dignified burial in a rich man's tomb.
Today we acknowledge the sorrow of
the people mourning and burying their murdered loved ones.

Lord Jesus Christ, today we remember your commission
to spread your hope, your peace, your love in the world.
Today we acknowledge with awe
your presence in all the people we are called to serve.

Lord Jesus Christ, today we remember your suffering,
the agony you endured because of the sins of the world.
Today we acknowledge with heartfelt gratitude
that you are our Lord, our Guide, and our eternal Friend. Amen.

Easter Eve

Waiting (Poetry)

Lord, we spend so much of our lives waiting.
Waiting eagerly for coming occasions of great joy.
Time passes steadily, minute by minute,
but for us it goes too slowly.

Lord, we spend so much of our lives waiting.
Waiting anxiously for pending situations of great pain.
Time passes steadily, minute by minute,
but for us it goes too quickly.

Lord, we spend so much of our lives waiting.
Waiting between crucifixion despair and resurrection joy.
Time passes steadily, minute by minute,
but for us it seems to have stopped still.

Lord, we spend so much of our lives waiting.
Waiting for you to deliver us from our troubles.
Waiting for you to astound us with your love.
Time passes steadily, minute by minute,
but for us there is never enough time for all your blessings.

Lord, we spend so much of our lives waiting.
Waiting for your coming with trumpet blast and angelic host.
Time passes steadily, minute by minute,
but for us you have come already, the unseen presence in our lives.

Lord, we spend so much of our lives waiting.
Help us instead to live in the moment,
aware of your signposts giving direction to our lives.
Time passes steadily, minute by minute,
but you are beyond time, and in you so are we.
Amen.

Easter Sunday

Our Lives are Shaped by Resurrection (Gathering)

Our lives are shaped by resurrection,
by our belief in the raising to glory
of the crucified one –
the anointed Son.

Our lives are shaped by resurrection,
by our trust in the mercy and grace
of the one who comforts and heals the broken –
the loving Father.

Our lives are shaped by resurrection,
by our hope in the creative power
of the one who restores life to the lifeless –
the energizing Spirit.

Because our lives are shaped by resurrection,
we encounter daily the mystery
of the communion the Infinite One seeks
with us – frail, finite, imperfect people.

Because our lives are shaped by resurrection,
we gather to honour the resurrected one,
acknowledging that
our lives are sustained by his life,
our hope is grounded in his love,
our future is secure in his keeping.

Because our lives are shaped by resurrection,
we desire that our worship of you
Holy God of all living,
reflect and be shaped by your Spirit of Life,
the eternal Spirit of resurrection. Amen.

Easter Comes to Us in Autumn (Poetry)

Easter comes to us in autumn
and with it the abundance of the harvest,
a profusion of sweet flavours and textures,
source of preserves for sustenance
and wine for cheer in days to come.
At Easter we recall gospel stories
that challenge and inspire us,
and provide soul food to nourish hearts and minds
and get us through the barren times.

Easter comes to us in autumn,
when leaves turn red and gold,
before shrivelled and brown they fall
from lofty heights to replenish the soil.
At Easter we tell the story of one
whose death overcame death,
one crowned with barbarous thorns not glistening gold
and draped in a red army cloak over bloody shoulders,
as soldiers mocked.

Easter comes for us in autumn,
when seeds mature and scatter
to lie hidden from view
dormant in the soil,
a promise of new life to come.
At Easter we remember the one lain
out of sight in a garden tomb,
awaiting the third day
and the new life to come.

Easter comes to us in autumn,
when the morning air has a chilly feel,
when rain falls on summer's parched lands
and we mark on calendars
the day when clocks are turned back to winter's time.
With ashes we begin Lent,
our journey of remembrance towards
the chill of rejection and the joy of resurrection,
when time was changed for all time, at Easter,
which comes to us each autumn. Amen.

ANZAC Day

Remembering the ANZACs (Poetry)

Matthew 24:6-7

Green grass now grows where once red poppies dared to flower,
and pastures now remove from view
the blood and mud of battle fields.
Pilgrims come from far away to walk on mown lawns reverently
between neat rows of white headstones, looking for a family name,
shedding silent tears and speaking, if at all, in hushed tones.
How quiet it is where painful screams and fear-filled yells,
the rat-tat-tat of gunfire and the deathly sound of exploding shells,
told of the chaotic horror and hideous suffering of war.

Here lie buried the uncles that did not come home,
the fathers that never saw their children's children,
and out there are the bodies never found,
dust returned to dust in foreign fields.
Young men whose names appear on plinths
in every town and hamlet in this southern land,
and are inscribed in faded gold on school honour rolls –
a young country mourning the loss of its young.
Now we look for them online
– name, rank, service number, date and place of death –
and find in their identity as ANZACs our national one.

Their colonial patriotism birthed by European nationalism,
they left these shores for good King George and the old country,
the place they had never seen yet referred to as "home."
They left with high hopes of quickly getting the job done,
dealing to the Hun, and having a great Boy's Own adventure.
We speak of their sacrifice as being for our freedom,
conveniently forgetting that at Gallipoli our side were the invaders
and the Johnny Turks the young men fighting to preserve freedom.

Each April a new generation gathers at dawn to salute the ANZACs
and to promise anew to immortalise them in memory.
We recite the Ode – "With the going down of the sun and in the morning,
we will remember them. We will remember them." But how?
Not as having fought the war to end all wars, which was their hope.
"You will hear of wars and rumours of wars," said Jesus.
"Nation will rise against nation and kingdom against kingdom."
Is it not to our shame and their dishonour that this is still true?
Did they not give their lives so that no one else would ever need to?

Home and Family Day

We Give Thanks for Families (Thanksgiving)

We give thanks for families;
for young families with growing children,
for mature families with grown up children,
for blended families with many children,
for extended families of multiple generations.
We give thanks for a world full of families.

We give thanks for fathers;
for young fathers excited and
daunted by their new responsibilities,
for mature fathers
enjoying the company of their adult children,
for fathers of blended families
entrusted with supporting another's children,
for grandfatherly fathers, a treasure to their children's children.
We give thanks for all the world's fathers.

We give thanks for mothers;
for young mothers raising children
with and sometimes without partners,
for mature mothers with wisdom
guiding the next generation,
for stepmothers and foster mothers
stepping in for birth mothers,
for grandmothers dispensing loving hugs
and sharing stories of days gone by.
We give thanks for all the world's mothers.

We give thanks for brothers and sisters,
for cousins and aunts and uncles,
for nanas and poppas and grandmas and grandpas,
and godmothers and godfathers,
and parents and step parents,
for young children and grown up ones.
We give thanks for all the world's families.

We give thanks for the family of the church;
for God our Father, Christ our Big Brother, the church our Mother,
and for all our siblings from every nation on earth.
We give thanks for all the world's families. Amen.

For Children and Their Families (Intercession)

John 6:5; Mark 9:36-37; 10:13-16

Father God may your loving-kindness
be reflected in our care of the children you bring into our lives;
within our families and in our churches.
As relatives, neighbours, teachers, preachers, passers-by,
may we treasure each young person we encounter,
the unattractive and unlovable no less than the beautiful and adorable.

May we love extravagantly like you,
not expecting anything in return.
Like a canopy of forest trees, together may we provide
shelter from the storms of life for the tender plants
growing beneath our outstretched limbs.
With the good things you so abundantly bestow upon us,
may we nourish and nurture the young ones you entrust to our care
and give them all they need to become what you desire them to be.

Jesus, you who took the lunch of a small boy of generous heart
and transformed it into a picnic meal for thousands,
combine and multiply our small gifts and bumbling efforts
and through them meet the needs of the world's hungry people.
Provide for the children needing the basics of life,
and for the adults starving for your words of life.
Take the little we have to offer, the little we are able to do,
and work a miracle for children living in poverty,
and for families living where there is famine and war.

Blow through the earth Holy Spirit,
the sweet fragrance of God's love for every human being.
Pour out your blessings on people without regard for race and creed.
Anoint with hope our children like those whom Jesus called to him,
the little ones his disciples would have sent away.
Enfold in love our infants like those Jesus cuddled in his arms
and said of such as these is the kingdom of God made. Amen.

Mother's Day

A Prayer for Mothers (Intercession)

Lord, we pray for mothers this Mother's Day.
We ask that you bless young mothers, new to the responsibility of caring for their much loved but very demanding babies.
Bless them with gentleness, energy and endurance, particularly when suffering the effects of sleep deprivation.

Lord we ask that you bless mothers in full-time employment, juggling the demands of employers and families, workplaces and homes.
Bless them with real quality time with their loved ones, and guilt free opportunities for refreshing solitude when required.

We ask you to bless stay-at-home mothers, needing the mental stimulation of adult conversation and challenged to find new ways of keeping their children amused.
Bless them with good friends to meet with regularly, and endless creativity to educate and entertain their little ones.

Lord, we ask you to bless solo mothers, having to be a parent twice over for their children, and oftentimes struggling to make ends meet.
Bless them with supportive champions to mentor their children, and sufficient income to meet their needs.

We ask you to bless foster mothers, who take into their homes and hearts troubled children.
Bless then with insightfulness and wisdom so that they may transform young lives through their loving care;

and we ask you to bless step mothers, whose presence in the lives of another woman's children can be resented.
Bless them with the qualities of kindness and patience, and may their sacrifices come to be recognised and appreciated.

Lord we ask you to bless mothers in war ravaged and famine afflicted places, who fearfully wonder if their children will even reach adulthood.
Bless them with peace and well-being, so they will know the joy of seeing their children's children.

We ask you to bless mothers whose children have died, for whom Mother's Day is a time of painful memories and sadness for a life cut short and memories never made.
Bless them with happy thoughts and the comfort and encouragement of a robust faith.

Lord we ask you to bless elderly mothers, now dependent on the good will and support of their adult children.
Bless them with loving children and grandchildren, respectful and caring, who graciously attend to the needs of those of advanced years.

Lord we don't want to forget those women who are not mothers themselves, for whom Mother's Day can be a painful celebration.
Bless them with recognition that as aunts, friends and teachers they are making a valuable and essential contribution to the raising of subsequent generations.

Lord God, we thank you for our own mothers and our grandmothers. We have been blessed by their instruction, comforted by their hugs, encouraged by their faith in us, and empowered by their love.
Lord, may your loving-kindness be evident through us, not only within our families but among all your children throughout the world.
In Jesus name we request this. Amen.

Call to Worship on Mother's Day (Gathering)

Today we celebrate families,
and the mothers who nurture them.

Today we celebrate discipleship,
and the church that nurtures us.

Today we celebrate the Holy One,
who unites us into one holy family;

and to whom we offer our humble praise
and heartfelt thanksgiving this day in this place,
as we gather together, your people,
listening for your voice in what is said, sung
and reflected upon during our hour of worship. Amen.

Mother's Day Blessing (Blessing)

May the Father who for Sarah, Elizabeth and Mary
worked the miracle of motherhood,
continue to do mighty deeds in and through your lives.
May the Son who made disciples
of the sisters Martha and Mary of Bethany
continue to encourage you by his gospel message.
May the Spirit who raised up the church
in which Lydia, Priscilla and Phoebe served,
continue to inspire you to do good works.
May the One who is Parent, Brother, and Comforter
bestow his bountiful blessings upon you this Mother's Day. Amen.

Winter

Winter's Lessons (Poetry)

Just as freshly fallen snow is beautiful in its whiteness
before it is crushed and muddied by human footprints,
so God your Spirit blankets the world with a loveliness
that somehow survives being trampled over.

Just as the flickering red and gold flames
of a crackling fire give forth the gift of warmth,
promoting a sense of well-being,
so God your Spirit of light and love
banishes from our lives all that is dark and chilly.

Just as the golden goodness of pumpkin soup,
the tasty pleasures of pickles and preserves,
and the heartiness of a Sunday roast,
nourish us with the fruits of an autumn abundance just past,
so God your Spirit bountifully provisions us
for the stormy seasons of our lives.

Just as camellias bloom
when frosts are many and flowers are few,
and buried bulbs poke up tender shoots through sodden ground,
hinting of a spring time blossoming just ahead,
so God your Spirit comes to us in times of loss
with signs of resurrection life to come.

God, we thank you for winter –
its pleasures and its challenges –
and for the wintry seasons in our lives.
Times when our restlessness is stilled,
times when reflection and meditation is required,
times when circumstances bring to remembrance...

That just as trees denuded of summer leaves
reveal their skeletal splendour for all to see,
silhouettes against grey skies and watery landscapes,
so God your Son, divested of his majesty,
came among sinful humanity to reveal your glory,

your never ending love and mercy,
by way of the cold inhumanness
and life sapping ugliness of the cross. Amen.

Pentecost

Lord God, Source of Eternal Light (Gathering)

John 1:1-5; 3:5-8, 16-17; 4:10-14; 7:37-39; Acts 2:1-4

Lord God, source of eternal light,
we come seeking illumination.
Lord God, the wind that blows through our lives,
we come seeking the Spirit's inspiration.
Lord God, the source of living water,
we come seeking refreshment at the
spring that gushes up to eternal life.

We have gathered together
knowing you are in our midst.
We have gathered together
listening for your voice.
We have gathered together
your people born to new life.

Open our minds
to understanding your word.
Open our mouths
in joyful praise and grateful prayer.
Most of all, open our hearts
to the Son who came into the world
not to condemn the world but to save it.

We acknowledge our failures
and seek your forgiveness of our iniquities.
We know our shortcomings
and seek your patience with our inadequacies.
We have come from our world to worship.
Send us back into your world to praise.

Bless this holy time O Lord.
In Jesus name we pray. Amen.

Spirit God (Gathering)

Genesis 1:2; Exodus 19:18 - 20:1-21; Psalm 78:14; 1 Kings 8:10-11;
Isaiah 6:1-4; Ezekiel 43:1-5; Malachi 3:1; Mark 1:9-13; Acts 2:1-4

Spirit God, hovering over a watery world,
ordering creation from primordial chaos,
clothing earth's nakedness with nature's abundance,
breathing your spirit life into our humanness;
shelter us under your motherly love,
transform our turmoil into tranquillity,
fill up our emptiness with your wisdom divine,
raise us aloft on the winds of eternity.

Spirit God, dwelling in pillars of cloud and of fire,
alighting on Sinai in flaming splendour,
thundering forth commandments of covenant,
sanctifying holy a nation of slaves;
guide us on journeys through barren wastelands,
help us climb mountains for encounters with you,
speak laws of love into our consciences,
make sacred a church of commonplace folk.

Spirit God, filling with glory Solomon's temple,
soaring heavenward on chariots of fire,
inspiring your prophets with visions that challenge,
promising the coming of the Davidic Messiah;
form from your people your present day temple,
transport us above our everyday thinking,
show us the ways of heaven on earth,
make of us true disciples of the Anointed One.

Spirit God, as a dove descending,
declaring beloved of the Father his Son,
driving the Christ into the wilderness,
inspiring rebuffs to the tempter's allures;
fly down upon us the blessing of peacefulness,
proclaim our membership of the family of God,
be there for us in our spiritual barrenness,
grant us release from the enemy's snares.

Spirit God, on Pentecost coming,
sounding like wind and appearing like fire,
descending upon the hundred and twenty,
bringing to birth the new covenant church;
bless our celebration of time that is holy,
full us with the joy that gives light to our lives,
be in our midst as we gather together,
proclaim in and through us the gospel of God. Amen.

We Experience the Spirit Moving (Gathering)

In earth's wild places and within the trappings of civilisation,
in moments of wonder inspired by nature and human creativity,
we experience the Spirit moving and sense your presence.
In familiar words that encourage and through acts of loving kindness,
said and done by those we know well
and by strangers who are not yet friends,
we experience the Spirit moving and sense your presence.
In moments of quiet prayer and meditation,
alone and listening for words whispered in our minds,
and in times of jubilant praise and worship,
singing along with the crowd in adulation,
we experience the Spirit moving and sense your presence.
These hints of you draw us to this place in response to you.
In our togetherness this Pentecost and during our worship here today,
we will experience the Spirit moving and sense your presence. Amen.

Pentecost Blessing (Blessing)

May the Spirit who hovered over the primordial water,
bringing into being abundant life on earth,
bring light and fruitfulness to our lives.
May the Spirit that appeared as a column of cloud and fire,
leading the Israelites through the wilderness,
lead us in our daily walk of faith.
May the Spirit that filled the first temple with glory,
and came with signs of power to the first church in Jerusalem,
fill us with God life, that we may be truly blessed.
May God, Father, Son and Spirit, be with us all
now and forever. Amen.

Pentecost Offering (Offering)

Giver of the resources of the bountiful earth,
giver of the hope of the gospel of peace,
giver of the gifts of the Holy Spirit,
loving Lord, to you we offer these our gifts in gratitude;
in the belief that even when they are small
you can use them effectively for the work of your church;
that the good news of Jesus,
first proclaimed long ago in Jerusalem on Pentecost,
will continue to go out into the world. Amen.

May We Dance (Poetry)

Sweet Holy Spirit, may we have the pleasure of dancing with you.
May we whirl round and round and round in giddy ecstasy,
in time to the rhythm of your great love song for humanity.
May the brilliance of your divine beauty overwhelm us,
and the fragrance of your heavenly perfume overpower us,
and in your arms may we dance on and on and on for all eternity.

Holy Spirit (Praise)

*Psalm 33:8-9; Genesis 1:2; Hosea 8:1; Exodus 3:2; 13:21-22; 40:34;
Kings 8:11; 18:38; 19:11-13; Isaiah 6:6; Mark 1:10-12; Matthew 17:1-5;
Acts 2:1012; Exodus 19:16-17*

Holy Spirit whispering through our lives
like the rustle of leaves in a summer breeze.
***Holy Spirit sweeping through our lives
like the force of a gale on a winter's day.***

You roared through the cosmos on Creation Day
speaking the universe into existence.
Then eons later you brooded over a planet
and out of stardust you brought forth life.

Holy Spirit fluttering through our lives
like the soft touch of a butterfly's wings.
***Holy Spirit swooping down upon us
with outstretched talons like a bird of prey.***

You were a burning bush that didn't burn up,
causing a shepherd to take notice of you.
You were a cloud of smoke and a column of fire
leading a people to their promised land.

Holy Spirit choosing to wander with a wandering people
covering the tabernacle with the cloud of your glory.
*Holy Spirit choosing to settle with a colonising people
making holy a temple by your holy presence.*

You were in the fire that consumed Elijah's sacrifice
and then in silence on Sinai you spoke loudly to him.
You were in the hot coals that touched Isaiah's lips
and through sages and prophets you are speaking to us.

Holy Spirit as a dove you descended on the Christ
driving him into the wilderness to be tested.
*Holy Spirit with divine brilliance you transfigured Jesus
and you commanded his disciples to listen to him.*

You blew into Jerusalem on the Day of Pentecost
manifesting yourself as flames of fire,
you set the world ablaze by equipping a people
to witness to Jesus in tongues not their own.

Holy Spirit once more your people are traversing
a wilderness that only you can lead us safely through.
*Holy Spirit bring us again to your holy mountain,
bring us once more to an encounter with you. Amen.*

Trinity Sunday

Lord We Come (Gathering)

Lord, we come, your people, reflections of your image.
We come to worship you, with words said and sung,
we come to hear you in scripture read and reflected upon,
we come once more to wrestle with the mystery of your being,
the one God who is three in one.

Lord, we seek to grow more perfectly in your likeness.
We seek to express more completely our deep devotion,
we seek to listen more receptively to your profound teaching,
we seek once more to wrestle with the mystery of our being
of such great importance to you, Triune God.

Lord, we hope to go representing you to all the world.
We hope to go, our deeds proclaiming our faithful dedication.
We hope to go teaching all, all that you have taught us,
disciple making disciples; and as we go, once more we wrestle with the
great commission to proclaim you Father, Son and Holy Spirit.

Be with us in our coming, be with us in our seeking and our going.
Be with us here today, and in all our tomorrows.
We ask in Jesus' name. Amen.

A Blessing for Trinity Sunday (Blessing)

You are the beloved of the life-giving Father,
the cherished of the resurrected Son,
and the comforted of the advocating Spirit.
May you be blessed throughout the week ahead,
experiencing the loving presence of God,
who is Father, Son and Spirit. Amen.

Disability Sunday

What We Truly Are (Petition)

We all have limitations.
Some have visible issues.
Many have hidden problems.
None of us is truly whole.
Only you God are without imperfections.

We all have possibilities.
Some we readily grasp.
Many we are yet to discover.
None of us is without abilities.
Only you God know our true potential.

We are all differently-abled.
Some things we find easy to do.
Many things we find difficult.
None of us are without challenges.
Only you God can do everything.

We all need a helping hand.
Encouragement is important.
Opportunities are essential.
None of us can flourish without support.
Only you God are not dependent on others.

We all get classified.
Some are called handicapped.
Others are described as impaired.
Many are assumed to be able-bodied.
None of us should be defined by labels such as these.
Only you God know who and what we truly are.

We all share in humanity's brokenness.
We all need to accept and be accepted.
We all need to forgive and be forgiven.
We all need to love and be loved.
Only you God can heal our defectiveness.
Only you can make us spiritually whole. Amen.

Ordinary Time (Any Time)

Only a Prayer Away (Poetry)

As we journey daily through our lives
we are glad we do not travel alone,
that you are beside us God unseen and unobtrusive
yet only a prayer away.

Providing strength when we are weak,
rest when we are weary,
comfort in times of hardship, hope when our faith falters,
and encouragement when our courage fails.

Although we stumble from time to time
and get side tracked into unprofitable ways,
and although negative attitudes slow our progress
and we persist with burdensome behaviours,
Lord you never leave us to struggle on alone.

Rather, you are ever loving, ever merciful.
You understand our inadequacies and forgive our misdeeds.
You are gracious in spite of our gracelessness.
Kind in spite of our spitefulness,
and gentle even when we lack empathy.

This way we are travelling
is not the route we would have chosen, Lord.
In trust we are walking pathways you lead us on,
guided in our pilgrimage by scripture our road map,
to the destination you have prepared.

As we travel, we give thanks
for the companions you have provided
to accompany us on this life-long journey,
and for those who share our joys and sorrows.
We give thanks for your constant presence Lord,
for being as close as a prayer away.

As you travel beside us,
teach us to become more like you God,
to love like you do without reservation,
to be merciful like you are without hesitation, and
to give of ourselves with unbounded generosity,
and help us to always remember
that you are as close as a prayer away. Amen.

God You Don't See as We See (Petition)

1 Samuel 16:7

God you don't see as we see.
You are not impressed by fortune and fame.
You know beauty is so very fleeting
and that charm can often be vain.

God you don't see as we see.
You look at what lies deep within,
at attitudes affecting our thinking,
leading to both virtue and sin.

God you don't see as we see.
So we ask that you give us insight,
to view our ways as you see them,
to delight in doing what's right.

God you don't see as we see.
So we desire to become more like you,
that we may be pleasing in your sight,
and see things the way that you do.

God you don't see as we see.
You see what we have become,
your family of beloved children,
redeemed by the death of your Son.

Prayer for Illumination (Illumination)

Life speaking God,
who sent Jesus,
the Word of Life into our lives;
who inspired men of old
to write prophecies to correct us,
psalms to inspire us,
proverbs to make us wise,
and gospels to encourage us.
Speak to us once more
through your scriptures read
and reflected on today. Amen.

Lord Heal Us of Our Blindness (Confession)

Lord, heal us of our blindness.
Not just our dimming eyesight,
the result of aging and disease,
but our spiritual blindness,
the result of self-absorption.

Lord, heal us of our blindness.
The blindness that doesn't see
when our words are hurtful,
when our actions are deceitful,
when our attitudes are harmful.

Lord, heal us of our blindness.
The blindness that doesn't see
when people are being wounded,
when people are being victimised,
when people are being damaged.

Lord, heal us of our blindness.
The blindness that doesn't see
the cruelty of gossip,
the abusiveness of dishonesty,
the harm of prejudice.

Lord, heal us of our blindness.
Give us the insight to see
the beauty of kind words,
the loveliness of good works,
the power of inclusive thoughts.

Lord, heal us of our blindness.
Help us to see as you see. Amen.

With Words of Encouragement (Commissioning)

Lamentations 3:22-23; Psalm 23:1-2; Luke 15:3-7; John 10:11-16

With words of encouragement and signs of deliverance,
God comes with assurance of His steadfast love and faithfulness.
Go from here out into the week ahead
knowing that you are cherished beyond measure,
and may the Shepherding God, Father, Son and Holy Spirit,
lead you to pastures green and waters still,
and seek you out when you get lost. Amen.

The God Who Sees (Thanksgiving)

Genesis 16:13

In periods of plenty and in times of deprivation
you are the God who sees.
The God who sees how we value the abundance.
The God who sees how we share when resources are scarce.

In periods of joyfulness and in times of sorrow
you are the God who sees.
The God who sees our gratitude for our happiness.
The God who sees our willingness to share another's burdens.

In periods of peacefulness and in times of conflict
you are the God who sees.
The God who sees how we seek to live in harmony.
The God who sees how we strive to end strife.

In periods of recreation and in times when we labour
you are the God who sees.
The God who sees how we are refreshed by our Sabbath rest.
The God who sees what we do with the talents we have.

In periods of boisterous companionship
and in times of silent solitude
you are the God who sees.
The God who sees how good and faithful a friend we truly are.
The God who sees how contemplative we can be when alone.

You are El-roi, the God who sees,
not as a scientist curiously observing an experiment,
nor as a spectator of the game of life,
but as a loving parent allowing us to play the ball our way,
but always cheering us on whether we are playing well or badly,
whether we are winning or losing.

You are El-roi, the God who sees.
The God who sees us in our wonderful moments,
sees us when things are going wrong.
The God who sees us in all our circumstances,
sees us in all our states of mind.
Most of all the God who sees us through loving eyes,
and always looks upon us with eternity in view. Amen.

The Limits We Place (Confession)

Philippians 4:13

In awe of you great God we offer up our praise,
and confess our sinfulness.
***We seek forgiveness Lord, for the limits we place on you
and the limits we place on ourselves.***

You call us to step out in faith. We ponder the likely consequences
of your call and decide you are asking too much of us,
forgetting that all things are possible
through the One who strengthens us.
***We seek forgiveness Lord, for the limits we place on you
and the limits we place on ourselves.***

God who is love, and who lovingly seeks
a relationship with all of humanity,
how often we fruitlessly struggle to grow your kingdom of love
by our own efforts alone, forgetting that it is your freely blowing Spirit
who sends forth your love into the world.
***We seek forgiveness Lord, for the limits we place on you
because of the limits of our thinking.***

God of inconceivable majesty and power
who cannot be contained within the universe,
how little we are in comparison to you,
yet how great our conceit when we think
we can determine what you can and cannot do,
and what can and cannot be.
***We seek forgiveness Lord, for the limits we place on you
because of the limits of our comprehension.***

In seeking your forgiveness Lord,
we also seek from you a greater faith.
A faith that will follow you,
even when the way ahead seems uncertain;
a faith that believes in your greatness
even though we cannot truly perceive your magnitude;
a faith that sees beyond present realities to future possibilities;
a faith like that required of Abraham and Sarah,
knowing that with you God there are no limits.
***Grant us your forgiveness Lord,
and empower us with your Spirit. Amen.***

In Search of Us (Thanksgiving)

Luke 15:1-7

Lord we speak of seeking your presence,
but it is you who search after us
to draw us into a relationship with you.

So it was with the Children of Israel,
whom you delivered from Egyptian slavery
to meet with you at a mountain in Midian.

So it was with the Babylonian exiles,
whom you restored to their homeland
to rebuild a temple in which to worship you.

So it was with Galilean fisher folk,
called to become the disciples of Jesus,
empowered by the Spirit to start the church.

So it was for the Pharisee Saul,
struck down by you on the road to Damascus,
commissioned to be your messenger to the nations.

We come seeking you, but it is you who seek and find us.
Always leading us during our wilderness experiences,
always with us during our exile and return experiences,
always teaching us during our discipleship experiences,
always equipping us for our mission experiences.
We confess that too often we ignore your leading.

Too often we are oblivious to your presence,
too often we are deaf to your teaching,
too often we insist on living our lives our way.
Like wayward sheep we have a tendency to stray,
but you are the Good Shepherd who seeks us out
and restores us to the protection of your sheepfold.

We speak of seeking your presence,
but in heartfelt gratitude we acknowledge
that it is not us who seek after you,
but you who search for us,
to draw us into an eternal relationship with you.
For this in humility we offer praise and thanksgiving. Amen.

Between this World and His Kingdom (Blessing)

May the God who comes alongside you,
Father, Son and Holy Spirit,
guide and protect you, inspire and encourage you,
bless and sanctify you, as disciples who travel
along the pathway on the razor edge
between this world and his glorious kingdom. Amen.

The Sound of Thunder the People Heard (Poetry)

John 6:1-14; 12:29; Matthew 9:9-13

The sound of thunder the people heard
was for Jesus the voice of God.
The small boy's lunch of fish and bread
was for Jesus a meal for the crowd.

The sinners despised by the Pharisees
were for Jesus the family of God.

Like the people who heard the thunder,
we aren't attuned to listening for God.
Like the disciples who anticipated hunger,
we lack faith in the provision of God.

Like the pious quick to judge others,
we overlook the loving-kindness of God.

We want to become more like Jesus
and hear like the way that he heard.
We want to see the impossible happen
as when he multiplied the fish and the bread.

We want to be successful in mission
and welcome many into the church.

God, open our ears to your teachings,
so we hear what you have to say.
Open our eyes to your blessings,
so we see how much you provide.

Open our minds to your loving
saints and sinners exactly the same.
Open our hearts to all people
and by our love your goodness proclaim. Amen.

Between Two Realms (Confession)

John 17:16-18

Merciful God,
we live straddled between two realms –
your kingdom and the societies of this world.
We live with divided loyalties,
confessing that we are more attuned
to the ways of the world than to your ways.
Your expectations appear demanding
and we find living up to them difficult.
We are acutely aware of our failures,
but we have the assurance of your forgiveness.

This gives us the outrageous confidence
to continue living this life of faith,
daily striving for increasing faithfulness.
But just living can be hard,
without taking on the challenge of living righteously.
We experience many frustrations.
We wish we didn't have our limitations –
physical, mental, spiritual.
We wish we were bigger, better,
and bolder servants of the eternal God.

Yet you call the little people to serve you.
People like us.
We who have no cause for pride,
no reason to have confidence in our own abilities.
People like us.
We who are all too aware of our many short-comings.
We do the best we can with what talents we have,
knowing how little our best efforts often are.
We tell ourselves we would do more if we could
and sometimes wonder if perhaps we could do more than we do.

Yet we know that we are the treasured ones,
loved and honoured by the king of heaven.
How astonishing we find this to be.
In our minds we shout out our gratitude,
but often only a whisper comes from our lips.
Even so we know we have been heard
and with thankfulness we offer our praise. Amen.

More of You and Less of Us (Confession)

You gave us dominion over your creation
to care for and protect all living things of land and sea.
Instead we have greedily exploited the earth's resources,
damaging and destroying its delicate ecosystems. *Forgive us.*

You made us in your image to live compassionately in community.
Instead we have fostered a culture of self-interest,
afflicting one another for personal gain. *Forgive us.*

You gave us a holy book to inspire our faith
and instruct us in abundant living.
Instead we have turned its teaching into oppressive rules
with which to judge and condemn those on the margins. *Forgive us.*

You gave us a gospel and a mission to take good news to the world.
Instead we have built buildings to settle down in and created faith
traditions that focused too much on ourselves. *Forgive us.*

God if we in the church are to live in harmony with creation,
if we are to become the loving community you desire us to be,
then in our thinking, our planning, our doing
there needs to be less of us and much more of you.

Only by the might of your Spirit, the power sustaining the universe,
can we change and live righteously, can we rightly discern
the scriptures and proclaim the gospel effectively.

We ask once more for your forgiveness, but also express our hope
that in future there will be far more of you and much less of us
in the way that we dwell in the world. Amen.

We Acknowledge Your Grace (Assurance)

God we acknowledge our weaknesses and are grateful that
your immense strength is constrained by your great compassion,
your just judgment is moderated by your gracious mercy,
you fierce anger is extinguished by your benevolent empathy.
We acknowledge our limitations and are grateful that
your love for us knows no limits, your generosity towards us
is beyond measure, your forgiveness of us is forever assured.
In humility and thankfulness we acknowledge your grace. Amen.

Lord We Gather (Gathering)

Lord we gather together today to hear
once more the story of your love for us.

We need to be frequently reminded
about how wonderful you are towards us,
and how precious we are to you,
because sometimes we forget this great truth.

We need to be reminded that your word cannot be broken,
that what you have promised will come to pass,
even though sometimes the waiting seems very long.

So, in the midst of our daily challenges,
foster within us an unshakeable faith in you,
and an unquenchable love for you.
Bless our worship here today. Amen.

You Alone (Gathering)

God you alone are absolute being;
we seek your gift of wholeness.

You alone have total comprehension;
we seek your gift of insight.

You are the only source of revelation;
we seek your words of wisdom.

You alone make possible complete healing;
we seek to feel your compassionate touch.

You make the darkness of night and the sunlight of day;
we desire to be people of illumination.

You give honey its sweetness and lemon its tang;
we yearn to savour the fruits of your Spirit.

You perfume flowers with their fragrance
and imbue decay with its pong;
we offer you the incense of our prayers.

You make the stillness of silence and the movement of sound;
we present our praise in music and song.

In and through our worship today let us become
a little more whole, a little more insightful,
a little more wise, and a little more compassionate.

Help us to be a little more like you.
Bless our worship today we pray. Amen.

Precious in Your Sight (Confession)

Loving God, we praise and thank you
that each of us is equally precious in your sight.
You gave ancient Israel a law, applying to king and peasant alike,
and you commanded compassion for the weak and vulnerable,
the widows, the orphans, the refugees.

Loving God, we confess that all too often we have put our own interests
above the need of others,
and have not done all we could have done for those in desperate
circumstances. *Father, forgive us.*

Loving God, we praise and thank you
that each of us is equally precious in your sight.
When you came to us as one of us you fellowshipped with outcasts,
healing their infirmities, forgiving their sinfulness,
inviting them to join you in your kingdom.

Loving God, we confess that all too often in many subtle ways we exclude
those who aren't like us, those we aren't comfortable around,
we disapprove of those we think responsible for their own misfortune,
we denounce those whose sins are different from our own.
Jesus, forgive us.

Loving God, we praise and thank you
that each of us is equally precious in your sight.
Through your Spirit inspiring poets and prophets, songwriters and sages
you created scripture that calls us to live in loving harmony.

Loving God, we confess that all too often we have had a tendency of
turning your teaching into rules by which to burden one another,
into rules by which to judge one another,
into rules by which to justify our own self-righteousness.
Holy Spirit, forgive us.

Loving God, we praise and thank you
for the unfathomable depth of your love for us.
We thank you for your forgiveness.

In our worship today – through our praising, praying, preaching –
may we, yet again, get an impression of your greatness.
May we, yet again, express our heartfelt
gratitude for your incredible compassion.
Loving God, we praise and thank you
that each of us is equally precious in your sight. Amen.

A Community of Great Value (Gathering)

Wherever we are
we are always in your presence Lord,
and are always able to pray to you;
but when we come together Lord,
we value joining our voices together in prayer.

Whatever we are
we are always recipients of your grace Lord
and are always able to sing praises to you;
but when we come together Lord,
we value joining our voices together in song.

Whoever we are
we can always have access to your word Lord
and most of us are able to study it ourselves;
but when we come together Lord
we value hearing your scriptures expounded upon.

Today here we are
assembled once more to worship you Lord.
The chipped and cracked body of Christ,
defective but nevertheless precious to you.
For when we come together Lord
you form us into a community of great value to you. Amen.

With our Lips We Praise You (Gathering)

With our lips we praise you, O God.
Lips with which to speak of the astonishing beauty of your creation
and the wonder of your unending love.

With our minds we praise you, O God.
Minds to perceive the incredible depth of your compassion
and your way of justice and mercy.

With our hearts we praise you, O God.
Hearts to feel the great generosity of your beloved Son, Jesus
and to respond to him as faithful disciples.

We give thanks for the opportunity to gather here today
to sing your praises and to listen to your promises once more. Amen.

There can be No Answers without Questions (Confession)

There can be
no answers without questions,
no faith without doubt,
no hope without crisis,
no love without sacrifice,
no resurrection without a death.

Lord God,
when our curiosity expires,
our faith is sorely tested,
our hope grows dim,
our love is self-serving,
and we are no longer living fully
but allowing the cares of life to overwhelm us,
and the promise of resurrection to forsake us,
forgive us, and restore us.

Lord God,
help us ask the right questions
and accept that the right answers may be elusive.
Help us to acknowledge our doubts
and allow our faith to thrive in spite of them.
Grant us hope in times of difficulty
and gratitude in times of refreshing.
Help us to love as you love sacrificially
and to graciously accept the loving of others.

Show us how to live as resurrection people,
fully alive every moment you give us,
assured of the conquering of death
achieved by the risen Son of God. Amen.

How Wonderful (Thanksgiving)

God who seeks to befriend us,
how wonderful that you seek us out
even when we are indifferent to you,
even when we are in denial of you,
even when we are in rebellion against you.
How wonderful that you care for us
even though we sometimes care little about you.
We praise and glorify your name.

God who seeks to release us,
how wonderful that you seek to free us
from enslaving habits that control us,
from worries and fears that burdens us,
from persistent sins that trouble us.
How wonderful that you rescue us
even though we sometimes turn away from you.
We praise and glorify your name.

God who seeks to be in covenant with us,
how wonderful that you love us
even though we are often unfaithful,
even though we are often ungrateful,
even though we are often untrustworthy.
How wonderful is your forgiveness of us
when we need you to pass over our sins.
We praise and glorify your name.

God who seeks to be with us,
how wonderful is your presence.
We are thankful for your graciousness,
we are thankful for your kindness,
we are thankful for your gentleness.
How wonderful we have discovered you to be
in all the varied circumstances of our lives.
We praise and glorify your name. Amen.

"The harvest is plentiful, but the labourers are few" (Confession)

Matthew 9:37-38; Ephesians 4:11-13; 1 Timothy 2:4

Lord of the harvest, in your word we read
that you have equipped your people
with all the gifts necessary to sustain and edify the church.

Lord we look at our limitations and question
whether the claims made in scripture truly apply to us.
How can we meet all the needs to be met?
How can we accomplish all the work to be done?
The harvest is indeed plentiful, but the labourers are far too few.

Faced with the reality of a secular world,
an increasingly disconnected society, and numbers when small,
we wonder what possible difference we can make.
The task seems overwhelming
and we confess to being inadequate for it.

But this is your world, Lord, not ours.
It is your desire that all humanity come to a saving knowledge of you.
This is your church, Lord, not ours.
You determine the seasons of its growth
and the time when it lies dormant in fertile soil.

These are your fields we labour in, not ours.
It is your desire that seeds planted will germinate
and that a bountiful harvest be brought in.
All that you plan will come to pass.
Our task is to believe that this will be so.

For we acknowledge that
through our weakness your power is revealed,
through our smallness your greatness becomes apparent,
and that you bring about success where we only envisage failure.
We need to stop thinking and acting
as though this is our work, Lord, and not yours.

Replace our troubled thoughts by helping us to see that truly
all that is needed is provided,
all those who are needed are present,
all talents necessary are available;
and so help us to do your work
in this place, at this time, with these people
in accordance with your glorious plan. Amen.

Words of Assurance (Assurance)

When our faith proves fickle and deserts us
and we turn away from God,
the moment we confess our faithlessness
we are forgiven and cherished.

When in spite of good intentions
we behave in ways we shouldn't,
the moment we confess our wrongdoing
we are forgiven and cherished.

When relying on our own strength
we stumble and fall into sinfulness,
the moment we confess our transgression
we are forgiven and cherished.

Whenever we turn towards God
we are always forgiven and cherished. Amen.

For All You Have Done (Gathering)

For all that you have done for us,
for all that you are doing for us,
and for all that you will do for us,
God who was, who is, and who will always be,
Father, Son and Holy Spirit,

we offer you our humble praise
and heartfelt thanksgiving this day in this place,
as we gather together, your people,
listening for your voice

in that which is said and sung
during our hour of worship.
We have come seeking your blessing. Amen.

What a Privilege (Gathering)

What a privilege to come into the presence of God,
to worship in the house God has provided.

What an honour to venerate the Holy One
with prayers of praise and songs of exultation.

What a blessing to be disciples of the Christ.
Hearing his words, reflecting on their meaning.
Bless this gathering today and our worship we pray. Amen.

As Guests Invited (Gathering)

We come,
invited guests of the One
who calls disciples,
Israel's patriarchs and us friends.
From out of our diversity God is creating
one united holy community,
having a common faith and hope
and with love as the adhesive bonding us together.

We are a community of friends,
old friends and new friends,
sharing old memories and making new ones.
We are a community of torch bearers,
entrusted to hold high the Christ light
and run with it for a time in this place.

We are a community of worshippers,
who with words and in silence
pray to and honour the Holy One.
May our worship be an acceptable
sacrifice of praise to him this day. Amen.

God is Not Limited by Our Limitations (Blessing)

Philippians 1:6

Sarah became the matriarch of the Children of Israel
even though she was too old to have children.
Ruth became the ancestress of the Kings of Judah
even though marriage to a Moabite was forbidden.
Mary became the mother of the Christ
even though she had no husband.
Look to these and other examples and know
that God is not limited by our limitations.
Then go from here confident in the blessing of God,
Father, Son and Holy Spirit,
with the assurance that the good work
God has begun in and through you
will be accomplished to God's glory. Amen.

Another Week Has Passed (Gathering)

Lord, another week has past, and we gather as a congregation,
part of your great worldwide family of faithful ones.
Another week has past, and we come together
to sing praises to your name,
to hear once more your wondrous deeds proclaimed.
Another week has past, and we gather together
assured that your steadfast love and faithfulness
will continue to strengthen us today
and preserve us in the days ahead,
until another week has past and we come together
again to sing praises to your name,
and proclaim your gospel of unending love. Amen.

Blessing for Older Folk (Blessing)

May you only encounter friendly faces
and may you always have reason to smile.
May you only hear kindly words
and may your speech be always gracious.
May you only experience loving attitudes
and may your actions be always considerate.
May the God whose love for you is limitless
bless and protect you this and every day. Amen.

Well of Salvation (Gathering)

Isaiah 12:1-6

We come to the well of salvation,
to Jesus the Christ
the giver of living water,
the Spirit that sustains life eternal.

We come to the well of salvation,
to Jesus the Logos
the giver of wisdom,
the one who speaks the words of life eternal.

We come to the well of salvation,
to the body of Christ
the community of saints,
the church gathered today to worship
Jesus, the source of life eternal. Amen.

God Our Companion (Offering)

God our companion,
the generous giver of good gifts,
receive from us our gifts of love
presented to you for our fellow pilgrims -
for those travelling like us with you
on this adventure called life;
and for those travelling like us
but unaware of your presence.
Bless these offerings that through them
good may result and you may be honoured. Amen.

The Darkness of Our Doubts (Confession)

Lord, when the darkness of our doubts
robs us of the light of your promises;
when our focus on what we cannot do prevents us
from seeing what you can do through us;
when our vision becomes clouded with prejudices
so that we cannot see that we are being more
judgemental than conciliatory;
when we say what should not be said
and fail to say what needs to be said;
when we leave undone that which we should do
and do that which we should not;
when we forget about the commitments we have made;
when our faith becomes feeble and our courage fails;
when we find it hard to trust and difficult to obey;
Lord forgive us. Give us hope
by filling us with the assurance of your love
now and forever. Amen.

We Have Come (Gathering)

Isaiah 12:3; Revelation 19:7-9

We have come to be refreshed at the well of salvation.
We have come to be fed in the house of the Lord.
We have come to be chosen, a bride for the bridegroom.
We have been come to be invited
to the marriage supper of the lamb.

We have come to be blessed by the presence of God.
We have come to worship. Bless our worship we pray. Amen.

In this Humble Place (Gathering)

Lord God, we have not climbed up to Jerusalem
to the courtyards of Solomon's temple,
nor have we gathered under the soaring vaulted ceilings
of some medieval cathedral in an ancient city in Europe,
but rather we have come to this more humble
dwelling place for your spirit.

Like those who have gone before us,
some worshipping in places of greater grandeur,
others worshipping in tents or in the open air,
beside river banks and upon hill tops,
we have been drawn here
by the favour and honour you bestow upon us,
and by the faith and trust you instil within us.

Lord God, we come to worship, for how else could we respond
to your grace, your generosity, and your love.
Accept and bless our worship here today. Amen.

We Have Confidence in You (Confession)

Matthew 19:26; Philippians 4:13; Isaiah 40:6-8; Job 14:1-2

Lord we are quick to focus on our limitations
and forget your ability to overcome all the barriers in our way.

Lord we are quick to focus on anticipated difficulties
and forget your ability to support us during troubles that may occur.
Lord we are quick to focus on what can't be done
and forget that what is impossible for us is possible for you.

Forgive us our failure of faith and faithfulness.

Sometimes we do dream of doing great things in your name,
but acknowledge that even little things often seem too hard for us.

Remember our fragility.
Remember that we are like flowers that bloom for only a season.
All too quickly and too often we get battered by the winds
of discouragement and disappointment.

Without you there is no hope, there can be no lasting happiness.

We have confidence in you,
knowing your love for us never ends
and your willingness to forgive us never diminishes.

We have confidence in you,
knowing that we truly can do all things through you,
the one who strengthens us.

For your mercy and your grace, we praise and thank you
in the name of Jesus. Amen.

Much to Praise You For (Gathering)

Lord, even when things go wrong, we have much to praise you for.
Although the earth has been shaken and buildings broken,
yet we have a safe place to gather together to worship.
Although anger and strife tear apart families and communities,
yet we have a peaceful place in which to pray and praise.
Although too many poor go hungry
and too many rich lack spiritual nourishment,
yet we enjoy both the bounty of the earth
and the fruitfulness of your word.

Great are your works O God,
and we who study them delight in them.
So we gather here today to be challenged
by you and your word to us;
challenged to think outside ourselves,
challenged to act beyond ourselves,
challenged to be more than ourselves,
because we are a people in a covenant relationship with you.
Steady us when we stumble, Lord, pick us up when we fall,
and most of all teach us to always be focussed
on he who is the way to truth and life, Jesus the Christ.
With confidence we ask you to forgive us our failings
and to bless our worship of you this day. Amen.

Fling Open the Gates (Poetry)

Fling open the gates to our hearts Lord
and invite Compassion and Love to come in.

Fling open the gates to the church Lord
and bid Mercy and Kindness move in.

Fling open the gates of our hearts Lord
and chuck Intolerance and Prejudice out.

Fling open the gates of the church Lord
root Spite and Self-righteousness out.

Fling open the gates to your kingdom Lord
and allow the disdained and the marginalised in.

Open wide the gates to your kingdom Lord
when our actions attract people in,
but close tight the gates of your kingdom Lord
to the dogmas that shut people out. Amen.

Our Parenting God (Intercession)

Matthew 6:9-13

Our parenting God,
who is present throughout the universe,
may your name be honoured here on earth.
May your loving ways be followed
where we live and everywhere else.
May we share the resources you provide
so that the daily needs of everyone are met.
May we learn to be forgiving of others
so that we ourselves will be forgiven.
Shield us from trials beyond our endurance
and protect us from all forms of evil.
For your reign is powerful and glorious
and will last forever. Amen.

Like Sheep (Gathering)

Mark 6:30-44

Like sheep needing a Shepherd to lead them
to rich pastures and refreshing streams,
**we come seeking nourishment from your word God
and refreshing from your Spirit.**

Like hungry villagers following Jesus into the countryside
and disciples without the money to purchase food for them
**we have followed where you have led us Lord
and are hungry for what we ourselves can't provide.**

Like the miraculous feeding of a multitude
with only five loaves and two fish
**we need your Spirit to transform the little we can offer
into worship that is worthy of you, Great God. Amen.**

Refugee Sunday

Care for the Vulnerable (Intercession)

Exodus 22:21-22; Deuteronomy 27:19; Psalm 72:12-14; Isaiah 58:6-7, 10;
Malachi 3:5; Matthew 25:35; James 2:27

Throughout scripture we are exhorted to care for the vulnerable:
the orphan, the widow and the refugee.

Today Lord our world faces a great crisis of people
fleeing from homelands engulfed in a frenzy of killing and destroying,
and risking death to cross dangerous seas in overcrowded boats.
Too often they are turned away from the safe haven of a port,
or hungry and weary they trudge along tracks and railway lines,
finally reaching concrete walls and razor wire fences to keep them out
of lands where they are not wanted;
desperate men, women and children, all vulnerable, all refugees.

Throughout scripture we are exhorted to care for the vulnerable:
the orphan, the widow and the refugee.
Today Lord our world faces a great crisis.
While we talk about what to do with this mass of displaced people,
while we reduce human suffering to immigration quotas
and exhibit our racial and religious prejudices,
the drowning continues, the homelessness escalates
and in winter, cold and wet weather adds to the misery.

God, we need an end to the violence, the conflicts and
the racial, religious and politically inspired persecutions
that drive people from their homes.

Having sacrificed much and travelled far in hope of freedom,
all too often refugees end up living
as prisoners in over-crowded camps
with little hope of ever reaching a place of sanctuary.

God, we need an increase in compassion.
Help us open our hearts and our homes and our countries
to the broken-hearted and the displaced.
Firstly providing the food and shelter necessary for survival
and then the dignity that comes only from having an opportunity
to use knowledge and skills in meaningful work.

God, we need an end to all wars and a vast reconstruction
of the places that have been bombed to rubble.
Eventually, when it's safe to return, we need to help
those who desire it to find a way back to their homelands.

Help us to commit to providing on-going support
until this tragedy is but a chapter in history,
a fading memory of a time when
the world did respond to your exhortation
to care for the vulnerable:
the orphan, the widow and the refugee. Amen.

Out of the Bounty of Your Grace (Offering)

Out of the bounty of your grace and mercy towards us,
we bring gifts for those in need of our grace and mercy.

Out of the abundance of your kindness and justice to us,
we bring gifts for those in need of our kindness and justice.

Out of the richness of your blessings and love of us,
we bring gifts for those in need of our blessings and love.

Thank you for giving us the gifts we bring.

May these gifts, in cash and kind and by direct credit,
help bring healing to the wounded and mending to the broken,
so that the hope of the gospel goes out beyond this community
to where that hope is so greatly needed.

Bless these gifts we pray and those who have given them.
In Jesus' name. Amen.

Peace Sunday

What would it take? (Poetry)

Micah 4:3-4; Luke 6:27-36; Leviticus 19:18

What would it take for nations to pursue peace not war?
What would need to happen for peoples to beat their spears
into pruning hooks, their swords into ploughshares?
Would it require summits, alliances and treaties?
God arbitrating between warring factions?
Or something simpler?
Everyday people,
being honest and honourable,
merciful and kind,
and living in harmony with one another.
Loving their neighbour as themselves.

We Pray as People who Mourn (Intercession)

Matthew 5:4

Lord, we pray as people who mourn.
Mourn for all the people destroyed
through vile acts of terrorism and needless wars.
Mourn for all the people destroyed through
avoidable made-made accidents and catastrophes.
Mourn for all the people destroyed through corporate greed
and government corruption.

Lord, we pray for the people who mourn.
Those who mourn the loss of family members and friends,
mourn the loss of tribal lands and traditional life-styles,
mourn the loss of homelands and communities.
Mourn because they have been robbed, exploited,
displaced, or forced to become refugees.

Lord, we pray for the people who cause mourning.
The people with political power who send young people to war.
The people with twisted religious ideologies
who radicalise young people into becoming suicide bombers.
The people with commercial power who exploit the weak
for personal and corporate gain.
The people with industrial power who rape and pollute the earth.
We pray that they will see the hideousness of their decision making
and find better ways of resolving conflicts and generating wealth.

Lord, we pray as people who mourn.
Mourn because we feel helpless to change the world
away from paths that lead to violence,
away from paths that lead to suffering,
away from paths that lead to environmental disaster.

Lord, we pray as people who mourn.
Help us to find ways to support and encourage the distressed,
speak up in support of the oppressed, and be a voice for the voiceless, even
when we seem to be crying in the wilderness.

Help us to be guardians of the planet,
leaving room for all other living things.
Help us to be peacemakers, even when that means being troublemakers.
We pray as people who mourn,
we pray as people who expect to be comforted,
we pray as the people of your kingdom on earth. Amen.

As When You Walked on Earth (Intercession)

Lord Jesus, when you walked on earth
you experienced the injustice of corrupt leaders
and the name of God being invoked
for evil and not for good.
You felt the hunger of a hand-to-mouth economy.
You experienced intense pain and knew the suffering of the sick.
You felt the fierce strength of the storm
and the searing heat of summer.

Things have not changed since you walked on earth.
There are still wicked leaders
governing for their own aggrandisement,
rather than making sacrifices
to improve the welfare of their people.
There are still people doing atrocities in the name of God,
which is surely the greatest of blasphemies.

There is still a vast number of people – a staggering one billion –
living in abject poverty,
and once self-sufficient people,
now homeless and helpless,
are being forced to flee from the horrors of war and famine.
Diseases still cause suffering
and drug companies profit from people's afflictions.

Storms and other natural disasters
still bring havoc and suffering.
Lord Jesus, we pray that humanity
may learn to embrace your way of out-going love.
We pray for hearts and cultures to be changed,
so that no longer will it be as when you walked on earth. Amen.

Be People of Compassion, Mercy and Peace (Blessing)

Be people of compassion, mercy and peace,
who hunger and thirst for righteousness.
Be rich in God's Spirit and poor in your own;
and know that the God of compassion, mercy and peace,
the God who is righteous beyond compare,
the Father, Son and Holy Spirit,
blesses you and those you love with his presence
this day and every day throughout eternity. Amen.

We are Challenged to be Merciful (Confession)

*Matthew 6:14, Matthew 7:1-2, Luke 6:35-36, Ephesians 2:8; 4:32,
Philippians 2:3-4, Romans 5:8; 15:5, Mark 10:45.*

We are challenged to be merciful;
to forgive others,
acknowledging our own need of forgiveness.

*We are challenged to be merciful;
to refrain from judging;
recognising that the standards we apply to others
also apply to ourselves.*

We are challenged to be merciful;
to respond with generosity towards the mean of spirit,
knowing that we too have a tendency towards
being selfish and self-serving.

*We are challenged to be merciful
and we confess that too often instead
we are self-righteously hard hearted. Forgive us.*

We are challenged to be gracious;
to act compassionately towards others,
acknowledging that we also are dependent on grace.

We are challenged to be gracious;
to be sensitive to the feeling of others;
recognising our own need to be always treated kindly.

We are challenged to be gracious;
to uphold the dignity of others,
not allowing our dreams to destroy theirs,
knowing how deeply we too desire
to be successful and respected.

We are challenged to be gracious
and we confess that too often instead
we are self-righteously hard hearted. Forgive us.

We are challenged to be loving;
to treasure each and every person however contemptible they seem,
acknowledging our own sinfulness and longing to be valued.

We are challenged to be loving;
to support and encourage others
recognising our own need to be cherished and nurtured.

We are challenged to be loving;
to give of ourselves for the benefit of others;
knowing our dependence on the benevolence of God
and the generosity of his creation.

We are challenged to be loving
and we confess that too often instead
we are self-righteously hard hearted. Forgive us.

In being challenged to be merciful, gracious and loving,
we acknowledge our need to be transformed.
We, who are being formed in your image,
merciful, gracious, and loving God,
recognise that we need nothing less than the miracle of
becoming increasingly like you.

We know that only by becoming
more and more merciful, gracious and loving,
will we become less self-righteously hard-hearted.
We who have been challenged,
seek to be the recipients of your mercy, grace and love.
We ask that you hear our prayer. Amen.

Today We Light the Christ Candle (Candle lighting)

Today we light the Christ Candle
in honour of the One who brings light to the world.
Lord bring light to all who are in places of darkness.

Today we light the Christ Candle
in honour of the One who gives abundant life.
Lord protect all whose lives
are threatened by violence and famine.

Today we light the Christ Candle
in honour of the One who redeems the world.
Lord deliver the world from evil, and us from complacency.

Today we light the Christ Candle, in honour of the One who revealed the Father and sent the Spirit to be our Advocate.
Today may our worship be pleasing to the Triune God. Amen.

Lay Preachers' Sunday

Lay Worship Leaders (Thanksgiving)

From many places and situations
to congregations known and new
come servants of the church
giving time and talents
to lead worship.

Not clergy with titles
and ecclesiastical garb,
but people for whom
the priesthood of all believers
is more than a nice sentiment.

People who bring from
classrooms and kitchens,
factories and farms,
offices and workshops,
life experiences
varied and insightful
to lead worship.

All service is ministry,
whether behind the scenes
where no one sees
or up front on the stage
in the sight of all.

All service is acknowledged,
all service is appreciated,
none more than any other,
but once a year on this Sunday
we gratefully express our thanks to God
for the lay people who come among us
to lead worship. Amen.

Father's Day

God our Father (Offering)

God who comes to us as Father
giver of all good gifts,
we come to you as children
sharing the bounty you have blessed us with.
Take these small tokens of our love and gratitude
and use them to spread the gospel of love
to those dwelling in this place at this time. Amen.

A Prayer of Lament for Fathers (Intercession)

Today we pray for fathers.
Fathers living where earthquakes have struck
mourning for beloved children buried in the rubble;
fathers living where bombs have been dropped
mourning for beloved children buried in the rubble.

Today we pray for fathers.
Fathers trying to keep their children safe
from rising flood waters engulfing houses;
fathers trying to keep their children safe
from roaring wild fires consuming homes.

Today we pray for fathers.
Fathers working long hours for little pay
to feed and clothe and educate their children;
fathers enduring lives of hardship and sacrifice
so that their children may live better lives.

Today we pray for fathers.
Fathers who are forced to take up arms
to protect the lives of their children;
fathers who suffer the degradation of war
so that their children may one day know peace.

We live in a prosperous and privileged land,
a safe place which should be infused with happiness,
where fathers are free to teach and nurture
and children are free to learn and play.
Yet even here there are fathers who struggle
to provide for their children's needs,
and fathers who know the pain of separation
and of being estranged from their children.

Today we pray for fathers.
God we bring before you all people suffering tragedy,
those who have lost love ones to the forces of nature,
those who have lost love ones to the evils of humankind.
We know that among those who mourn are many fathers.

Today we pray for fathers.
For all fathers, in all their circumstances,
for prosperous fathers and fathers who are poor.
We pray that you will help us find and put into practice
ways of supporting fathers and strengthening their families;
that you may use your church to bless fathers. Amen.

Spring

Spring Warming (Poetry)

The sun is warming the earth.
Kowhai is flowering,
birds are nesting,
spring bulbs burst into bloom.

Beauty is warming our hearts.
Trees are blossoming,
bees are buzzing,
flowers perfume the earth.

Spring is warming our souls.
Gardens are growing,
lambs are frolicking,
new life is surging forth.

God is warming our lives
Hope is budding,
love is growing,
faith is changing the world.

In Spring (Gathering)

Song of Solomon 2:10-15

In spring we give thanks for creation,
for the wonder and diversity of life.
In spring we thank God for the splendour
of all he has made on the earth.

In spring we remember the scripture
telling us when winter is past,
comes a time for joyfully singing
and for hearing God's loving voice.

Spring Flower Service

In Spring We Come to God with Praise (Thanksgiving)

In spring, when life begins to stir with renewed vigour,
released from the grip of winter's chilly weather,
we come to you God with praise.

Praise for the warming earth
and for the warming of our spirits.
Praise for the blossoming trees
and for the flowering of our hope.
Praise for the dawn chorus of bird song
and for each new day we greet with joy.

In spring,
when new life full of vibrancy and loveliness
lavishly bursts forth upon the earth,
we come to you God with praise.

Praise of you the great Creator
who made spring a season of glorious splendour.
Praise of you the extravagant Father
who shares with us a world of astonishing beauty.

Praise of you the Promise Keeper,
who gives us this annual reminder that
the cold, dreary, winter times of our lives
will be overcome by the delight of resurrection life.

In spring you remind us once more
that, "the time of singing has come."
So in spring we come to you God,
with hearts full of praise, and with gratitude
for the cheerful, colourful seasons of our lives. Amen.

Season of Creation

Sky (Poetry)

Genesis 1:1-30; 9:12-17

Sky, blue canopy covering earth,
an optical illusion of azure beauty,
window through which warming sun
brings light and life,
revealing colour in the world.
Orb rising and setting,
painting with hues of red and gold.

Sky, place of clouds fluffy white
like floating fantasy castles,
and dark, menacing, coming with
lightning flashes, rumbling thunder.
Swept along by wind, symbol of spirit,
dispensing rain, hail, snow,
quenching thirsty land,
overflowing rivers rushing seaward.
Rainbow, sign of covenant,
a promise of better weather.

Sky, sole realm of feathered creatures
until hot air balloons took us aloft.
Now as high as Himalayan geese fly
jets planes leave wisps of vapour trails,
on journeys towards adventures yet to come.
In ancient times mariners looked heavenward
and plotted pathways through uncharted seas.

Sky, dressed in black velvet evening gown,
bejewelled with shining moon and glittering stars,
the vastness of the universe on display.
We remember and give thanks that
God created the sky and it is good.

We and the Earth Mourn (Confession)

We and the earth mourn for her lost children,
the species that no longer
scuttle or scamper through her forests,
flutter and fly high above her land,
splash and swim in her rivers and seas.
The planet and we have become so much poorer by their extinction.
God forgive us.

Forgive our foolish and wanton destruction of habitat,
sometimes from ignorance,
sometimes out of necessity,
but too often the result of our desires
being elevated above earth's needs,
our preference for economy over ecology,
as if life consisted of the accumulation of things
and bank balances can feed bodies and souls.

Forgive our careless spewing forth of toxic chemicals
onto land and into air and waterways,
the by-products of our industrial processes,
changing places of beauty teeming with life
into ugly, smelly death dealing wastelands.
Save the planet by changing us O God.

Give us the vision, the desire and the determination
to replace our self-focused living with lifestyles in harmony
with the world of nature whose care is our responsibility.
Help us to stop the destruction and repair the damage done
while there is yet time to save precious wild places
and threatened species.

Bless with wisdom and knowledge
all who are striving to save earth's endangered creatures,
some small and insignificant like snails,
others large and magnificent like whales,
and those who are working to protect
fragile and diverse ecosystems.
Grant them success we pray. Amen.

Life Giving God (Confession)

Life giving God who showers blessings upon us
through warm sunshine and gentle rain;
who sends pristine streams
rushing down from mountain snow fields,
springing up from hidden aquifers,
pouring into swelling rivers flowing seaward.
We praise you for the gift of water.

*We confess that we have poured pollutants into waterways,
turning life teaming places into foul smelling eyesores.
Forgive us, and help us change our polluting ways.*

Life giving God who showers blessings upon us
through the sweet sound of bird song carried on gentle breeze;
who has created an interconnected ecology of plants and creatures
in and around the rivers of our land.
We praise you for the gift of living things,
for insects, fish and water fowl.

*We confess that we have destroyed habitat
and threatened species
by damming rivers to feed our insatiable demand for energy,
and through draining rivers to water marginal land
to increase pastoral production,
in order to earn more dollars to buy things
we often don't actually need.
Forgive us, and help us to work in harmony with nature.*

Life giving God, you gave us dominion over the fish of the sea,
over the birds of the air,
and over every living thing that moves on the earth.
That dominion was not licence to exploit and destroy
but responsibility to tend and protect.

*We have failed miserably to care for your creation.
Transform us, O God,
through the power of your Spirit of Recreation,
so that our relationship with all the species on this planet,
including our own kind, may finally become
what your always intended it to be. Amen.*

God of the Storm (Poetry)

Genesis 1:2; Psalm 104; John 8:12; 4:14; 3:8; Ezekiel 19:19; 1:4-21

God of warm summer days and cold winter nights,
of spring flowering and autumn fruitfulness,
of new life blossoming in pastel shades
and the golden huge of dying foliage.
As day follows night, so summer follows spring
and winter comes after autumn in never ending succession.
From space debris you formed the tilted earth
and began its yearly solar orbit dictating the cycle of the seasons.
Over this world your spirit blew, brooding the birthing of life.
You are the God of the storm.

God of gentle breezes and howling winds,
of still waters and pounding waves,
of sunny weather and sudden squalls.
The earth spins, the jet streams roar,
lows replace highs, cyclones replace anti-cyclones,
blue skies become obscured by dark water-burdened clouds
and dust particles blown skyward fall back to earth as raindrops.
You set in motion these forces of weather,
forces that both destroy life and sustain it.
You are the God of the storm.

God of snow-born streams rushing down mountain sides,
to feed meandering lowland rivers,
to merge into moon moved oceans,
to evaporate to form clouds and fall as snow once more.
Likewise your spirit constantly flows
through every part of the cosmos.
Your compassion is in the caress of sea-cooled air
on a hot summer's day.
Your dominion is in the chilling bitterness of a winter gale.
Your righteous rage reflected
in the rushing waters of the rising flood.
You are the life giver and the life taker.
You are the God of the storm.

God called the Light of the world,
the ever gushing spring of Living Water,
the Spirit that blows wherever it wills
and achieves whatever it desires.
Your voice is as the thunder and your presence as lightning.
Galaxies of fiery stars are pale reflections of your splendour.
The hurricane merely hints at your power.
Freshly fallen snow poorly reflects your purity,
and the cloaking sandstorm whipped up by dessert winds
only whispers of your covering presence.
You inhabit all that lives and dies,
during fine days and when the rain falls.
You are the God of the storm.

God the Creator (Poetry)

God the creator, who made the cosmos,
set galaxies swirling, from stardust formed us.
Your glory and might are on nightly display
in moon, stars and planets of the Milky Way.

God the lawgiver, who rules the cosmos,
with laws for all things, and commandments for us.
Although from our eyes you are always concealed,
yet now through our science you are being revealed.

God the life giver, who fills the cosmos,
who brought cells to life, and breathed life into us.
You started the process by which came to be
a wonderful world of biodiversity.

God the observer, who views the cosmos,
who looks upon earth, and who contemplates us.
You see how our actions are causing great harm
to earth's ecosystems which is raising alarm.

God the redeemer, who loves the cosmos,
most truly our Saviour because you love us.
Forgive us our sins and please change us we pray
that we may start living in accord with your way.

For the Victims of Climate Change (Intercession)

Merciful, life giving God, we pray on behalf of the people
who look up at blue skies and long for storm clouds,
who look down at parched ground and long for well-watered fields,
who view dry, shrivelled plants and live in fear of famine.
We pray for life restoring rain in draught stricken places.

Merciful, life giving Lord, we pray on behalf of the people
who look up at storm clouds and long for blue skies,
who look aghast at mudslides and long for stable land,
who view the flood waters rising and live in fear of drowning.
We pray for sunshine and dry land in flood prone places.

Merciful, life giving Spirit, we pray on behalf of the people
who look up at billowing smoky clouds and long for clear skies,
who hear the crackle of the encroaching fire and long for silence,
who view the red of the flames and fear being consumed by them.
We pray for the protection of life and property where wild fires roar.

Merciful, life giving God, we pray on behalf of the people
who hear the howl of the wind
and long for the whisper of a gentle breeze,
who fear the energy of the hurricane
and the destructive power of the tornado.
Who see the approaching whirlwind and fear being swept up by it.
We pray for the protection of people sheltering from the tempest's fury.

Merciful, life giving Lord, we pray on behalf of the people
who suffer the most from climate change.
The people who lives, lands, homes and livelihoods
are at the mercy of the violent forces of nature.
So many of these people are the world's poorest,
living in draught prone, flood prone, cyclone prone places.
We pray for your protection of people impacted by climate change.

Merciful, life giving Spirit, we pray on behalf of all people everywhere.
May each of us do all in our power, be that only a little
or be that much, to reverse the damage
we each have done to the world that you have made.
Help us to start living in harmony with nature and with one another.
Help us to cease actions that destroy that we may stop being destroyed.
This we ask in Jesus' name. Amen.

We Remember (Gathering)

Creator God of a universe
that is beyond our imagination in its vastness,
we remember that you are also the One
who treasures the little people of the world.

Creator God of the living earth,
that is beyond our comprehension in its complexity,
we remember that you are also the One
who cherishes the simple people of the world.

Creator God of vistas great and small,
breath taking in their beauty,
we remember that you are also the One
who cares for the plain people of the world.

We come this day to worship you.
We aren't the big people in society;
the important ones, the influential ones, the rich and famous,
but we are your people, the people who you love,
and for whom you sent your son that we may be delivered
from all that would separate us from you.
Accept and bless our worship today we pray, in Jesus name. Amen.

St Francis of Assisi Day

Thanksgiving for Companion Animals (Thanksgiving)

We thank you for the animals who live with us as pets,
sharing their lives with us and giving their affection to us,
playing with us, and being a constant source
of amusement and delight.
Bless us with the knowledge and ability
to keep them safe and well and happy,
and bless them with contentment.
May they be confident of our devotion
and our commitment to their well-being.
They enrich our lives, may we enrich theirs.
We thank you for our companion animals
who bring us so much pleasure. Amen.

Social Justice Sunday

We Pray for the Excluded (Intercession)

We pray for the excluded:
for those struggling with brain malfunction.
May they receive the encouragement and support they need,
and may the stigma of mental illness be eliminated.

We pray for the excluded:
for those struggling with addiction.
May they receive the encouragement and help they need,
for the bonds of their dependency to be broken.

We pray for the excluded:
for those in prison and those on probation.
May they receive the encouragement and support they need
to learn from past mistakes and be accepted back into the community.

We pray for the excluded:
for the hungry and the homeless.
May their basic human needs of food and shelter be provided
that they may live with dignity whatever their personal inadequacies.

We pray for the excluded:
for the lonely and isolated.
May they receive the acceptance and friendship they need
so that they may enjoy having someone to talk to.

We pray for the excluded:
for the sick and disabled.
May they receive the acceptance and assistance they need
to overcome the difficulties caused by their disabilities.

We pray for the excluded:
for the refugee, fleeing for safety.
May they receive the help and support they need
that they may find a new home and a new hope.

We acknowledge grace giving God
that we also have a part to play in drawing the excluded
back into the circle of your family on earth.
Help each of us to reach out in love to others,
and may our collective loving bring transformation
in the lives of the excluded.
This we pray in Jesus name. Amen.

We are Overwhelmed by Suffering (Intercession)

We are overwhelmed by suffering.
Not so much our own suffering,
nor the suffering of family and friends,
although these problems are painful and pressing
and cause us to cry out to you urgently for a way of release.

Rather we are overwhelmed by the suffering of
so many in our super-connected world,
brought to our attention daily through the technology of
live news broadcasts, no longer just headlines filtered by time.
Stories with graphic pictures
that show the human toll of storms, fires, earthquakes,
wars, suicide bombings, mass shootings.
Stories that convey the heartache of those who mourn
following road crashes, drownings, tragedies in the mountains.

We are overwhelmed by suffering.
The suffering of people in far-away places
and the suffering of people who are our neighbours.
We can't cope with this constant barrage of suffering.
Our hearts are in danger of becoming hardened by tragedy.
For ourselves and for others we offer up prayers of lament.

We are overwhelmed by suffering.
We feel helpless but can be grateful
for the people making a difference, doing what we cannot do;
the rescue workers, the fire fighters, the medical people,
the justice seekers and the peace keepers.
We admire the people speaking up against iniquity and inequality.
For them we offer up prayers of thanksgiving.

We are overwhelmed by suffering, and we cry out for your comforting
of the affected, the afflicted, the abandoned,
of those that moan and those that mourn.
We cry out for a better world for the victims of evil.
For them we offer up prayers of intercession.
We hold before you the world's suffering people,
the victims of war crying out for peace,
the fleeing refugee crying out for a home,
the enslaved child crying out for freedom.
For them we offer up prayers for deliverance.

We hold before you the world's suffering people.
Those who just want the earth to stop shaking,
the fires to stop burning, and the wind to stop blowing,
the rain to come and the crops to start growing,
the rain to cease and the flood to stop rising.
For them and for all we offer up prayers of hope,
in the belief that our words do indeed make a difference,
that you have endless love and care for this world
that is overwhelmed with suffering. Amen.

Those Whom You Never Forget (Intercession)

Matthew 5:3-10

Lord we pray for the poor and the meek,
those we know you have a special love for.
We pray that they don't hunger and thirst for the necessities of life.
We pray that their voices be heard, their concerns addressed,
and where their lands contain rich resources
they not be robbed of its bounty by multi-nationals.
We pray that in this world of adulation of the wealthy and powerful
you will protect the poor and the meek
and that we remember those whom you never forget.

Lord we pray for those who suffer and mourn,
those we know you have great compassion for.
We pray that their suffering be alleviated, their mourning comforted.
We pray for those whose love ones were victims of
deliberate catastrophes like terrorism and war
and unintended ones like traffic crashes and work-site accidents.
We pray that in this world of idolisation
of military and industrial power and unrestrained exploitation,
you will champion the cause of those who suffer and mourn
and that we remember those whom you never forget.

Lord we pray for those being persecuted for righteousness sake,
those we know you have a high regard for.
We pray that their desire for truth and justice be met.
We pray for journalists jailed for exposing corruption, activists reviled for
resisting evil, and believers persecuted for worshipping you.
We pray that in this world of moral confusion, you will encourage those
being abused for their righteous convictions
and that we remember those whom you never forget. Amen.

Words (Intercession)

We pray for those who are the victims of warmongering words.
Words that arise from an overly zealous patriotism
which advocate the path to conflict rather than the ways of peace.
Such words lead to unimaginable destruction and suffering.
We pray for the end of conflict between the peoples of our world.

We pray for those who are the victims of hateful words.
Words that distort an ancient faith from a way of living in harmony with
divinity to a way of bringing suffering to humanity.
Such words deceive young jihadists and kill their victims.
We pray for the end of religion-inspired violence in our world.

We pray for those who are the victims of deceiving words.
Words that make promises never intended to be kept,
words that make shady business propositions look promising,
words that promote products that don't work as claimed.
Such words steal both money and peace of mind.
We pray for the end of corruption in our community.

We pray for those who are the victims of bullying words.
Words spoken deliberately to hurt and cause harm
to subordinates in a work place, to students at school,
to people on the receiving end of emails and texts
and messages on social media.
Such words destroy self-esteem and can lead to suicide.
We pray for the end of bullying in real space and cyberspace.

We pray for those who are the victims of vicious words.
Abusive words spoken where they should never be said
in homes that should be havens of tranquillity,
to family members who should be precious beyond measure.
Such words leave scars long after mere bruises and abrasions have healed.
We pray for the end of domestic violence in our homes.

We pray that we may be the speakers of kindly words.
Words that encourage the downhearted, words that promote
healing in the hurting, words that express empathy and compassion.
Such words build up rather than tear down,
nurture rather than destroy.
We pray for the outflowing of loving words into our world.

Lord, hear our prayer, and transform our world
that our speaking may be for good and not for evil.
We speak these words in Jesus' name. Amen.

Transformed World (Intercession)

We pray for a transformed world;
where children can play free of fear of falling bombs,
where children can grow strong free of famine and disease,
where children can learn at school
free of racial and gender discrimination.
We pray for a transformed world where all our children can be free.

We pray for a transformed world;
where families live in harmony free from domestic strife,
where workers labour happily free from exploitation,
where people live free from the pain of prejudice and persecution.
We pray for a transformed world where all people can be free.

We pray for a transformed world;
a world where peace breaks out instead of war,
a world where generosity is common and greed is rare,
a world where water is plentiful and pure, and air fresh and clean.
We pray for a transformed world where we all can be free.

We pray for a transformed church;
which is more than a social gathering for a weekly worship fix,
which is more than a club for the spiritually like-minded,
which is more than the religious wing of a political movement.

We pray for a transformed church
that the grace of Jesus makes free.
We pray for a transformed church
which refrains from castigating the weak
but speaks powerfully to those in power,
which doesn't focus on petty theological differences
but is unified in Christ,
which is inclusive not judgemental, gentle not harsh.
We pray for a transformed church that in imitating Jesus is made free.

We pray for a transformed world,
and we pray that that transformation begins with us.
Help us to truly be the salt that flavours the world
with tolerance and compassion.
Help us to be the light that exposes falsehood and corruption.
Help us to be the ointment that heals the wounds of the suffering.
Help us to bring the water that quenches the world's thirst for justice.
Help us to prepare the food that nourishes the spiritually famished.
Help us to live the Jesus way, embracing his truth that sets all people free.

We pray that our world be set free from all that burdens it.
We pray that we be set free from all that burdens us.
We pray for transformation, globally, locally, individually.
We pray, and we have faith in the efficacy of our prayer.
In Jesus name. Amen.

We say, "This is not our doing." (Confession)

We praise you Lord
for instilling within humankind a spirit of adventure,
for the Abrahams of this world who left familiar places
and said goodbye to family and friends,
and then embarked on precarious journeys to far off lands,
with faith that somehow their migration would work out well.
We thank you for ancestors who traversed mighty seas
to come to this land which we call our home today.

We praise you Lord
for instilling within humankind a spirit of curiosity,
for the desire to know how things work
and why things are the way they are.
We thank you for scientists and explorers whose discoveries
have helped us better understand the universe,
thereby greatly enriching our mental landscape
and giving us a glimpse of your great majesty.

We praise you Lord
for installing within humankind a spirit of creativity.
For painters and sculptors, writers and musicians
who cause us to see differently the ordinary and everyday,
and for builders and engineers, and the makers of things
who create the fabric of our everyday lives,
the cities we live in and the objects we accumulate.

But, we confess to you Lord
that our adventuring has not been all good.
Too often it has led to conquest and colonisation
and the subjugation of indigenous peoples.
We say, "This was not our doing,
we didn't rob anyone of their land and their dignity;"
but to the extent that we lack empathy with the oppressed
and fail to do the small things we can do
to right past and present wrongs, we are guilty.
Forgive us and change us.

We confess to you Lord
that our scientific enquiry has not been all good.
Too often our learning has given us greater ability
to cause untold suffering to people,
and to the environment we share with other living things.
We say, "This is not our doing, we aren't makers of armaments,
or producers of toxic substances;"
but to the extent that we fail to do the small things we can do
to foster harmony and protect the earth's ecosystems
we are guilty.
Forgive us and change us.

We confess to you Lord that our creativity has not been all good.
Too often our culture has descended into the decadent and obscene.
Our construction has destroyed landscapes and habitats.
Our consumerism has led to vast rubbish dumps.
We say, "This is not our doing, we aren't the setters of fashion
and the moguls of industry;"
but to the extent that we fail to do the small things we can do
to uphold the ethical, the pure and the beautiful,
and are happy to purchase, then throw away things we don't need,
we are guilty.
Forgive us and change us.

You made us in your image with minds
that are enquiring and creative. We praise you for this,
and for the beautiful world in which we live.
So we pray for the wisdom, conviction and courage
to exercise a dominion of care over this your planet,
our home which we share with a multitude of creatures
suffering because of our actions.
Forgive us and change us,
so that we may live in harmony with one another
and with all other living things. Amen.

We Live in a World that Needs to Know You (Intercession)

We live in a world where people kill themselves to kill others.
We pray for healing for the victims of terrorist attacks
and for the repentance of those with a distorted understanding
of what is required of a true believer.

We live in a world where homes are places of danger
and families are damaged and dysfunctional.
We pray for deliverance for those who experience domestic violence
and for the repentance of those with a distorted understanding
of what is required of a partner or spouse.

We live in a world where children are exploited,
abused, mistreated and even murdered.
We pray for the protection of children whose trust is being betrayed
and for the repentance of those with a distorted understanding
of what is required of a parent or carer.

We live in a world where people are trafficked,
tricked and then trapped into servitude and prostitution.
We pray for the liberation of those deceived and enslaved
and for the repentance of those with a distorted understanding
of what is required of people who make promises.

We live in a world where people are exploited
working very long hours for very little pay.
We pray for support for those who struggle to meet basic needs
and for the repentance of those with a distorted understanding
of what is required from businesses and bosses.

We live in a world where rulers are addicted to power
and corrupt regimes are robbing their peoples.
We pray for the emancipation of those under the control of brutal
dictatorships and for the repentance of those with a distorted
understanding of what is required of governors
and those exercising judicial authority.

We live in a world of warmongering governments
and those who prosper from the manufacture of armaments.
We pray for the protection of those caught up in conflicts
and for the repentance of those with a distorted understanding
of what is required of those with military might.

We live in a world which has forgotten the rule
that the only way to true freedom and happiness
is to treat every person with respect and dignity –
to do unto others what we would have them do unto us.
We live in a world that needs to know you.
We live in a world that needs to repent. Amen.

Our Golden Images (Confession)

Exodus 20:4; 32:1-4; Psalm 4-5; Isaiah 40:19-20

Lord, we are easily distracted by the baubles of modern living.
We're enamoured with our smart phones
and other electronic gadgets.
We embrace with enthusiasm self-service checkouts in supermarkets
and do-it-yourself teller machines in banks,
and more and more our shopping is done on-line;
all of which disconnects us from our fellow humans
for the sake of saving salaries and supposedly time.
These are our golden images intended to make living easier for us
but which in fact makes us increasingly isolated from one another.

Lord, we are very concerned about the degradation of the earth.
but we have great confidence in our ability to
develop technologies to mitigate
the effects of our consumerism,
without requiring us to give up our love of things
or change our ways that are leading to
depletion, destruction and pollution.
These are our golden images intended to change our situation
but which in fact provide us with excuses for not changing ourselves.

Lord, we are troubled by the rough sleepers
and the beggars that litter our streets.
We are distressed by stories of the homeless living in cars,
and accounts of children going hungry to school,
but we believe in the effectiveness of the market place
to reward fairly everyone according to their efforts.
We tell ourselves that the destitute could
lift themselves out of deprivation if they but tried a bit harder.
These are our golden images intended to create a strong economy
but which in fact leads to an underclass of impoverished people.

We are vaguely aware that our confidence maybe misplaced,
that our technological progress while wonderful
may not be our saviour after all.
That our consumption of things while appealing
may not be a wise use of the earth's resources.
That our business processes while generating wealth
may enrich some beyond measure while exploiting others.
Having made all these into golden images
we find ourselves lost in a wilderness of
self-absorption and self-gratification.

Lord, we thank you for our technological advances.
Help us use them in the service of your kingdom
for the betterment of all humanity,
and forgive us for having worshipped our technology.
Lord we thank you for shops full of a vast array of goods to buy.
Help us to make purchases in the service of your kingdom
for the betterment of all humanity,
and forgive us for having worshipped our possessions.
Lord we thank you for a robust economy.
Help us to use our wealth in the service of your kingdom
for the betterment of all humanity,
and forgive us for having worshipped our bank balances and GDP.

The knowledge that enables our technological developments
is your gracious gift to us.
The materials and minerals from which our stuff is made
is your gracious gift to us.
Our ability to live in communities, to run businesses and
trade goods between one another is your gracious gift to us.
Let us cease using your blessings
to create golden images to worship instead of you.
Rather let us use these blessings for the work of your kingdom
and bring about an end to the
exploitation of the earth's fragile ecosystem
and the exploitation of the earth's fragile people.
In Jesus name, we seek this miracle. Amen.

All Saints

We Pray for the Persecuted Church (Intercession)

Lord God we pray for the persecuted church.
For those who suffer because of their faith in you
at the hands of people from other faith traditions
unable to conceive that the God who created such a vast universe,
and populated our world with such a variety
of creatures and plants and peoples,
can be worshipped in many different ways.
Bless those who worship the Christ in Islamic lands.

Lord God we pray for the persecuted church.
For those who suffer because of their faith in you
in lands where humans imagine they can do without you,
places where churches not sanctioned and controlled by the state
face great danger every time they assemble in secret;
places where churches are not permitted in any form
and people imprisoned for their beliefs
are tortured and murdered for their faith in you.
Bless those who believe in the Christ in authoritarian lands.

Lord God we pray for the persecuted church.
For those who suffer because of their faith in you,
like those dismissed from academic institutions
when their science leads them to a belief in you;
those in situation where they are often ridiculed and belittled
as unenlightened and irrational because of their faith in you;
those who live at odds with people whose pride
in human intellect has deceived them
into embracing a belief system that believes in nothing.
**Lord bless ourselves and others in a world
becoming increasingly secular and intolerant.
Help us to remain loyal to the Christ in our neo-pagan lands. Amen.**

For the Mission to Come (Offering)

We remember the saints who have gone before us,
and their generosity which we now benefit from.
We pray for the saints who come after us,
and give gifts to benefit the mission to come.
Your blessing is sought on these gifts of love Lord.
May your gospel go out to the world. Amen.

Giving Thanks for Those Who Serve in the Church (Thanksgiving)

We express our gratitude for all who serve the church.

We give thanks for administrators:
for presbyters, deacons and elders,
and clerks and secretaries, and committee members.

We give thanks for musicians:
for those who write hymns and those who sing songs,
for those who lead choirs and those who play strings,
for pianists and organists, guitarists,
and those who keep rhythm on drums.

We give thanks for those who lead worship:
for clerics and lay preachers, and lay worship teams,
for those who read scriptures and those who pray prayers,
and those who deliver encouraging sermons.

We give thanks for mentors:
for Sunday school teachers, for youth groups leaders,
and the hosts of home groups;
for teachers and preachers, and for scholars and writers,
and for all who inspire and educate your church.

We give thanks for carers:
for those who go visiting, and those who run errands,
for those who stock food banks, and those serving in op shops,
for those who encourage, and for those who pray.

We give thanks for helpers:
for greeters who welcome, for ushers who guide
for cleaners and flower arrangers, and those who serve coffee,
for caterers and fund-raisers, and those doing outreach.

We give thanks for all who serve the church,
especially for those who serve unseen and unacknowledged.
We express our gratitude for those who serve,
and we seek God's blessing upon them all. Amen.

A Cloud of Witnesses (Poetry)

Hebrews 12:1

Children come trick or treating dressed in ghoulish costumes,
expecting sweet treats from neighbours,
not appreciating the extortion implied.
Just another imported custom, or so their parents believe,
not knowing that this is the day when the church honours its dead.
That great cloud of witnesses that surround us,
the martyrs, the sinners and saints,
who have completed their part of the relay
and have passed on the faith batten to us;
expecting us to run with perseverance
the race that is now ours to win,
and to faithfully pass on the gospel
to generations yet to run.

Reign of Christ Sunday

A Call to Worship the King (Gathering)

We come into the presence of the king;
the creator king, lord of the universe,
the saviour king, servant to his servants,
the redeemer king, his life our purchase price.

We come into his presence to worship.
We are drawn into the presence of the king:
the rabbi king, the teller of stories,
the prophet king, the maker of promises,
the priestly king, the divine mediator.

We are drawn into his presence to worship.
We are always in the presence of the king:
the guiding king, who shows us the way to go,
the traveller king, who is with us wherever we go,
the forgiving king, who pardons our sins as we go.

We are always in his presence to worship.
We give thanks to the king in whose presence we dwell:
the loving king, inspiring us to love like him,
the faithful king, calling us to have faith in him,
the righteous king, instilling within us the virtue in him.
We give thanks and we praise and we worship him. Amen.

We Remember (Confession)

Isaiah 9:6-7; Hebrews 12:22

We remember that the Holy One, the Christ,
is the Prince of Peace,
and we his people are to be people of peace.
Too often, however, we allow strife to prevail.
Forgive us.

We remember that the Holy One, the Christ,
is the Wonderful Counsellor,
and we his people are to be people of wisdom.
Too often, however, we are foolish in our ways.
Forgive us.

We remember that the Holy One, the Christ,
is the Everlasting Parent,
and we his people are to be a compassionate, caring people.
Too often, however, we are more selfishly childish
than generously childlike.
Forgive us.

We remember that the Holy One is the Mighty God,
the promised child on whose shoulders
the government of God rests,
and who rules with fairness and justice.
Too often, Sovereign Lord, we act in judgemental ways
that are neither fair nor just.
Forgive us.

Though we are unworthy,
we know that we are citizens of a heavenly Jerusalem,
and that our king is merciful.
We praise and give humble thanks Sovereign Lord
for your never ending loving kindness;
and we pray for the coming on your kingdom in its fullness,
when the world will know unending peace. Amen.

Sovereign Christ (Intercession)

Sovereign Christ, we pray for your kingdom to grow
That peace will break out in place of war
That justice will defeat corruption
That compassion will overpower contempt
That love will conquer hate.

Sovereign Christ, we pray for your kingdom to grow
That hunger will be consumed by plenty
That housing will abolish homelessness
That healing will overcome hurtfulness
That hope will demolish despair.

Sovereign Christ, we pray for your kingdom to grow
That education will expel ignorance
That truth will expose deceitfulness
That wisdom will sweep away foolishness
That faith will be stronger than doubt.

Sovereign Christ, we pray for your kingdom to grow
That harmony will overwhelm division
That integrity will supplant duplicity
That liberty will replace captivity
That God's ways will be lived on the earth.

Sovereign Christ, we pray for your kingdom to grow. Amen.

Scripture Index

About the Author

Joy brings to her writing a love of literature and a love of scripture. In the 1970s she graduated with an honours degree in English from the University of Canterbury, and in the 1990s she studied part-time for the Bachelor of Theology degree from the University of Otago, graduating in December 2004.

Soon after Joy began to be asked to lead worship for her home congregation and then for other congregations, learning how to do so by trial and error and with helpful advice offered by those sitting in the pews. This experience convinced her of the importance of resourcing lay worship leaders for the task they are requested to undertake.

Joy has served on the executive committee of the New Zealand Lay Preachers Association, including in the role of President. She is a member of the Village Presbyterian Church in Christchurch. Joy is now retired after a thirty-one year career with the Christchurch City Council, in the discipline of road safety education.

She is married to David Aitken, without whose support her lay preaching ministry could not happen.

• • •

Also now available:
Prayers for Southern People:
Poems and Prayers for Christian Worship and Devotions

Print: Soft cover, B/W text, 286 pages, 6" x 9"
eBooks: PDF, ePub, Mobi formats

This extensive new collection includes many types of liturgy: • Opening / Gathering • Candle lighting • Praise / Thanksgiving • Intercession • Confession • Illumination • Offering dedication • Blessing • Commissioning • Meditation.

The 326 entries are divided into three parts:
1. The Liturgical Year; 2. The Season of Creation;
3. Social Themes.

Includes a comprehensive Table of Contents and a full Scripture Index.

Order at **www.philipgarsidebooks.com**